M2M IoT
Complete Self-Assessment Guide

The guidance in this Self-Assessment is based on M
and standards in business process architecture, desi.... ....u quality
management. The guidance is also based on the professional judgment
of the individual collaborators listed in the Acknowledgments.

Notice of rights

Trademarks

Table of Contents

About The Art of Service

The Art of Service, Business Process Architects since 2000, is dedicated to helping stakeholders achieve excellence.

Defining, designing, creating, and implementing a process to solve a stakeholders challenge or meet an objective is the most valuable role… In EVERY group, company, organization and department.

Unless you're talking a one-time, single-use project, there should be a process. Whether that process is managed and implemented by humans, AI, or a combination of the two, it needs to be designed by someone with a complex enough perspective to ask the right questions.

Someone capable of asking the right questions and step back and say, 'What are we really trying to accomplish here? And is there a different way to look at it?'

With The Art of Service's Standard Requirements Self-Assessments, we empower people who can do just that — whether their title is marketer, entrepreneur, manager, salesperson, consultant, Business Process Manager, executive assistant, IT Manager, CIO etc... —they are the people who rule the future. They are people who watch the process as it happens, and ask the right questions to make the process work better.

Contact us when you need any support with this Self-Assessment and any help with templates, blue-prints and examples of standard documents you might need:

http://theartofservice.com
service@theartofservice.com

Acknowledgments

This checklist was developed under the auspices of The Art of Service, chaired by Gerardus Blokdyk.

Representatives from several client companies participated in the preparation of this Self-Assessment.

Our deepest gratitude goes out to Matt Champagne, Ph.D. Surveys Expert, for his invaluable help and advise in structuring the Self Assessment.

In addition, we are thankful for the design and printing services provided.

Included Resources - how to access

Included with your purchase of the book is the M2M IoT Self-Assessment Spreadsheet Dashboard which contains all questions and Self-Assessment areas and auto-generates insights, graphs, and project RACI planning - all with examples to get you started right away.

How? Simply send an email to
access@theartofservice.com
with this books' title in the subject to get the M2M IoT Self Assessment Tool right away.

You will receive the following contents with New and Updated specific criteria:
- The latest quick edition of the book in PDF
- The latest complete edition of the book in PDF, which criteria correspond to the criteria in...
- The Self-Assessment Excel Dashboard, and...
- Example pre-filled Self-Assessment Excel Dashboard to get familiar with results generation
- ...plus an extra, special, resource that helps you with project managing.

INCLUDES LIFETIME SELF ASSESSMENT UPDATES

Every self assessment comes with Lifetime Updates and Lifetime Free Updated Books. Lifetime Updates is an industry-first feature which allows you to receive verified self assessment updates, ensuring you always have the most accurate information at your fingertips.

Get it now- you will be glad you did - do it now, before you forget.

Send an email to **access@theartofservice.com** with this books' title in the subject to get the M2M IoT Self Assessment Tool right away.

Your feedback is invaluable to us

If you recently bought this book, we would love to hear from you! You can do this by writing a review on amazon (or the online store where you purchased this book) about your last purchase! As part of our continual service improvement process, we love to hear real client experiences and feedback.

How does it work?
To post a review on Amazon, just log in to your account and click on the Create Your Own Review button (under Customer Reviews) of the relevant product page. You can find examples of product reviews in Amazon. If you purchased from another online store, simply follow their procedures.

What happens when I submit my review?
Once you have submitted your review, send us an email at review@theartofservice.com with the link to your review so we can properly thank you for your feedback.

Purpose of this Self-Assessment

This Self-Assessment has been developed to improve understanding of the requirements and elements of M2M IoT, based on best practices and standards in business process architecture, design and quality management.

It is designed to allow for a rapid Self-Assessment to determine how closely existing management practices and procedures correspond to the elements of the Self-Assessment.

The criteria of requirements and elements of M2M IoT have been rephrased in the format of a Self-Assessment questionnaire, with a seven-criterion scoring system, as explained in this document.

In this format, even with limited background knowledge of M2M IoT, a manager can quickly review existing operations to determine how they measure up to the standards. This in turn can serve as the starting point of a 'gap analysis' to identify management tools or system elements that might usefully be implemented in the organization to help improve overall performance.

How to use the Self-Assessment

On the following pages are a series of questions to identify to what extent your M2M IoT initiative is complete in comparison to the requirements set in standards.

To facilitate answering the questions, there is a space in front of each question to enter a score on a scale of '1' to '5'.

1 Strongly Disagree

2 Disagree

3 Neutral

4 Agree

5 Strongly Agree

Read the question and rate it with the following in front of mind:

**'In my belief,
the answer to this question is clearly defined'.**

There are two ways in which you can choose to interpret this statement;
1. how aware are you that the answer to the question is clearly defined
2. for more in-depth analysis you can choose to gather evidence and confirm the answer to the question. This

obviously will take more time, most Self-Assessment users opt for the first way to interpret the question and dig deeper later on based on the outcome of the overall Self-Assessment.

A score of '1' would mean that the answer is not clear at all, where a '5' would mean the answer is crystal clear and defined. Leave emtpy when the question is not applicable or you don't want to answer it, you can skip it without affecting your score. Write your score in the space provided.

After you have responded to all the appropriate statements in each section, compute your average score for that section, using the formula provided, and round to the nearest tenth. Then transfer to the corresponding spoke in the M2M IoT Scorecard on the second next page of the Self-Assessment.

Your completed M2M IoT Scorecard will give you a clear presentation of which M2M IoT areas need attention.

M2M IoT
Scorecard Example

Example of how the finalized Scorecard can look like:

M2M IoT
Scorecard

Your Scores:

BEGINNING OF THE SELF-ASSESSMENT:

CRITERION #1: RECOGNIZE

INTENT: Be aware of the need for change. Recognize that there is an unfavorable variation, problem or symptom.

In my belief, the answer to this question is clearly defined:

5 Strongly Agree

4 Agree

3 Neutral

2 Disagree

1 Strongly Disagree

1. What are the business objectives to be achieved with M2M IoT?
<--- Score

2. What prevents you from making the changes you know will make you a more effective M2M IoT leader?
<--- Score

3. For your M2M IoT project, identify and describe the

business environment, is there more than one layer to the business environment?
<--- Score

4. Who else hopes to benefit from it?
<--- Score

5. Will new equipment/products be required to facilitate M2M IoT delivery, for example is new software needed?
<--- Score

6. What should be considered when identifying available resources, constraints, and deadlines?
<--- Score

7. What do you need to start doing?
<--- Score

8. What else needs to be measured?
<--- Score

9. Think about the people you identified for your M2M IoT project and the project responsibilities you would assign to them. what kind of training do you think they would need to perform these responsibilities effectively?
<--- Score

10. Can management personnel recognize the monetary benefit of M2M IoT?
<--- Score

11. Are there M2M IoT problems defined?
<--- Score

12. What are the expected benefits of M2M IoT to the business?
<--- Score

13. Is it clear when you think of the day ahead of you what activities and tasks you need to complete?
<--- Score

14. What training and capacity building actions are needed to implement proposed reforms?
<--- Score

15. Will M2M IoT deliverables need to be tested and, if so, by whom?
<--- Score

16. How much are sponsors, customers, partners, stakeholders involved in M2M IoT? In other words, what are the risks, if M2M IoT does not deliver successfully?
<--- Score

17. Does your organization need more M2M IoT education?
<--- Score

18. What vendors make products that address the M2M IoT needs?
<--- Score

19. Are controls defined to recognize and contain problems?
<--- Score

20. How can auditing be a preventative security measure?

<--- Score

21. How are the M2M IoT's objectives aligned to the organization's overall business strategy?
<--- Score

22. As a sponsor, customer or management, how important is it to meet goals, objectives?
<--- Score

23. Will it solve real problems?
<--- Score

24. Who defines the rules in relation to any given issue?
<--- Score

25. Have you identified your M2M IoT key performance indicators?
<--- Score

26. What situation(s) led to this M2M IoT Self Assessment?
<--- Score

27. Who needs to know about M2M IoT?
<--- Score

28. What problems are you facing and how do you consider M2M IoT will circumvent those obstacles?
<--- Score

29. How do you take a forward-looking perspective in identifying M2M IoT research related to market response and models?
<--- Score

30. Do you know what you need to know about M2M IoT?
<--- Score

31. How are you going to measure success?
<--- Score

32. How do you identify the kinds of information that you will need?
<--- Score

33. Consider your own M2M IoT project, what types of organizational problems do you think might be causing or affecting your problem, based on the work done so far?
<--- Score

34. How do you assess your M2M IoT workforce capability and capacity needs, including skills, competencies, and staffing levels?
<--- Score

35. How does it fit into your organizational needs and tasks?
<--- Score

36. Does M2M IoT create potential expectations in other areas that need to be recognized and considered?
<--- Score

37. What information do users need?
<--- Score

38. When a M2M IoT manager recognizes a problem,

what options are available?
<--- Score

39. What is the smallest subset of the problem you can usefully solve?
<--- Score

40. What does M2M IoT success mean to the stakeholders?
<--- Score

41. Are there any specific expectations or concerns about the M2M IoT team, M2M IoT itself?
<--- Score

42. Are there recognized M2M IoT problems?
<--- Score

43. Will a response program recognize when a crisis occurs and provide some level of response?
<--- Score

44. What tools and technologies are needed for a custom M2M IoT project?
<--- Score

45. What would happen if M2M IoT weren't done?
<--- Score

46. Who had the original idea?
<--- Score

47. What are your needs in relation to M2M IoT skills, labor, equipment, and markets?
<--- Score

Add up total points for this section:
_____ = Total points for this section

Divided by: _____ (number of
statements answered) = _____
Average score for this section

Transfer your score to the M2M IoT
Index at the beginning of the Self-
Assessment.

CRITERION #2: DEFINE:

INTENT: Formulate the business problem. Define the problem, needs and objectives.

In my belief, the answer to this question is clearly defined:

5 Strongly Agree

4 Agree

3 Neutral

2 Disagree

1 Strongly Disagree

1. How do you keep key subject matter experts in the loop?
<--- Score

2. Are approval levels defined for contracts and supplements to contracts?
<--- Score

3. Is the M2M IoT scope manageable?

<--- Score

4. Are there any constraints known that bear on the ability to perform M2M IoT work? How is the team addressing them?
<--- Score

5. How would you define M2M IoT leadership?
<--- Score

6. Have the customer needs been translated into specific, measurable requirements? How?
<--- Score

7. Are there different segments of customers?
<--- Score

8. Is M2M IoT required?
<--- Score

9. Has the improvement team collected the 'voice of the customer' (obtained feedback – qualitative and quantitative)?
<--- Score

10. What baselines are required to be defined and managed?
<--- Score

11. Are roles and responsibilities formally defined?
<--- Score

12. Is the scope of M2M IoT defined?
<--- Score

13. Do the problem and goal statements meet the

SMART criteria (specific, measurable, attainable, relevant, and time-bound)?
<--- Score

14. Are different versions of process maps needed to account for the different types of inputs?
<--- Score

15. Is the improvement team aware of the different versions of a process: what they think it is vs. what it actually is vs. what it should be vs. what it could be?
<--- Score

16. Is M2M IoT currently on schedule according to the plan?
<--- Score

17. Is full participation by members in regularly held team meetings guaranteed?
<--- Score

18. Is M2M IoT linked to key business goals and objectives?
<--- Score

19. Is there a critical path to deliver M2M IoT results?
<--- Score

20. Has a team charter been developed and communicated?
<--- Score

21. In what way can you redefine the criteria of choice clients have in your category in your favor?
<--- Score

22. When is the estimated completion date?
<--- Score

23. How will variation in the actual durations of each activity be dealt with to ensure that the expected M2M IoT results are met?
<--- Score

24. Is there a M2M IoT management charter, including business case, problem and goal statements, scope, milestones, roles and responsibilities, communication plan?
<--- Score

25. Have all basic functions of M2M IoT been defined?
<--- Score

26. When was the M2M IoT start date?
<--- Score

27. Are business processes mapped?
<--- Score

28. How can the value of M2M IoT be defined?
<--- Score

29. What are the record-keeping requirements of M2M IoT activities?
<--- Score

30. Are required metrics defined, what are they?
<--- Score

31. Is the team sponsored by a champion or business leader?
<--- Score

32. What are the compelling business reasons for embarking on M2M IoT?
<--- Score

33. Have specific policy objectives been defined?
<--- Score

34. Who are the M2M IoT improvement team members, including Management Leads and Coaches?
<--- Score

35. When are meeting minutes sent out? Who is on the distribution list?
<--- Score

36. What customer feedback methods were used to solicit their input?
<--- Score

37. How would you define the culture at your organization, how susceptible is it to M2M IoT changes?
<--- Score

38. In what way can you redefine the criteria of choice in your category in your favor?
<--- Score

39. What about when your context is not so simple?
<--- Score

40. Is the team adequately staffed with the desired cross-functionality? If not, what additional resources are available to the team?

<--- Score

41. What are the dynamics of the communication plan?
<--- Score

42. Are improvement team members fully trained on M2M IoT?
<--- Score

43. How often are the team meetings?
<--- Score

44. If substitutes have been appointed, have they been briefed on the M2M IoT goals and received regular communications as to the progress to date?
<--- Score

45. Context: where, when, who and why?
<--- Score

46. What constraints exist that might impact the team?
<--- Score

47. What are the Roles and Responsibilities for each team member and its leadership? Where is this documented?
<--- Score

48. Does the team have regular meetings?
<--- Score

49. How is the team tracking and documenting its work?
<--- Score

50. Is the current 'as is' process being followed? If not, what are the discrepancies?
<--- Score

51. Is the team equipped with available and reliable resources?
<--- Score

52. What is the meaning of success in this context?
<--- Score

53. Are audit criteria, scope, frequency and methods defined?
<--- Score

54. What critical content must be communicated – who, what, when, where, and how?
<--- Score

55. Are team charters developed?
<--- Score

56. What are the boundaries of the scope? What is in bounds and what is not? What is the start point? What is the stop point?
<--- Score

57. Has the M2M IoT work been fairly and/or equitably divided and delegated among team members who are qualified and capable to perform the work? Has everyone contributed?
<--- Score

58. Has everyone on the team, including the team leaders, been properly trained?

<--- Score

59. What defines best in class?
<--- Score

60. Are accountability and ownership for M2M IoT clearly defined?
<--- Score

61. Is a fully trained team formed, supported, and committed to work on the M2M IoT improvements?
<--- Score

62. What specifically is the problem? Where does it occur? When does it occur? What is its extent?
<--- Score

63. Is data collected and displayed to better understand customer(s) critical needs and requirements.
<--- Score

64. Has a project plan, Gantt chart, or similar been developed/completed?
<--- Score

65. What would be the goal or target for a M2M IoT's improvement team?
<--- Score

66. Have all of the relationships been defined properly?
<--- Score

67. Are task requirements clearly defined?
<--- Score

68. Are customers identified and high impact areas defined?
<--- Score

69. Is there regularly 100% attendance at the team meetings? If not, have appointed substitutes attended to preserve cross-functionality and full representation?
<--- Score

70. Has the direction changed at all during the course of M2M IoT? If so, when did it change and why?
<--- Score

71. Is there a completed SIPOC representation, describing the Suppliers, Inputs, Process, Outputs, and Customers?
<--- Score

72. Is there a completed, verified, and validated high-level 'as is' (not 'should be' or 'could be') business process map?
<--- Score

73. How was the 'as is' process map developed, reviewed, verified and validated?
<--- Score

74. Will team members perform M2M IoT work when assigned and in a timely fashion?
<--- Score

75. How does the M2M IoT manager ensure against scope creep?
<--- Score

76. How and when will the baselines be defined?
<--- Score

77. What key business process output measure(s) does M2M IoT leverage and how?
<--- Score

78. Has anyone else (internal or external to the organization) attempted to solve this problem or a similar one before? If so, what knowledge can be leveraged from these previous efforts?
<--- Score

79. Are customer(s) identified and segmented according to their different needs and requirements?
<--- Score

80. Is the team formed and are team leaders (Coaches and Management Leads) assigned?
<--- Score

81. Has/have the customer(s) been identified?
<--- Score

82. How will the M2M IoT team and the organization measure complete success of M2M IoT?
<--- Score

83. Who defines (or who defined) the rules and roles?
<--- Score

84. Will team members regularly document their M2M IoT work?
<--- Score

85. Do you all define M2M IoT in the same way?
<--- Score

86. What are the rough order estimates on cost savings/opportunities that M2M IoT brings?
<--- Score

87. Is it clearly defined in and to your organization what you do?
<--- Score

88. Has a high-level 'as is' process map been completed, verified and validated?
<--- Score

89. How did the M2M IoT manager receive input to the development of a M2M IoT improvement plan and the estimated completion dates/times of each activity?
<--- Score

Add up total points for this section:
_ _ _ _ _ = Total points for this section

Divided by: _ _ _ _ _ _ (number of statements answered) = _ _ _ _ _ _ Average score for this section

Transfer your score to the M2M IoT Index at the beginning of the Self-Assessment.

CRITERION #3: MEASURE:

INTENT: Gather the correct data.
Measure the current performance and
evolution of the situation.

In my belief, the answer to this
question is clearly defined:

5 Strongly Agree

4 Agree

3 Neutral

2 Disagree

1 Strongly Disagree

1. How will success or failure be measured?
<--- Score

2. Is data collection planned and executed?
<--- Score

3. What are your customers expectations and
measures?
<--- Score

4. What measurements are possible, practicable and meaningful?
<--- Score

5. What evidence is there and what is measured?
<--- Score

6. The approach of traditional M2M IoT works for detail complexity but is focused on a systematic approach rather than an understanding of the nature of systems themselves, what approach will permit your organization to deal with the kind of unpredictable emergent behaviors that dynamic complexity can introduce?
<--- Score

7. How do your measurements capture actionable M2M IoT information for use in exceeding your customers expectations and securing your customers engagement?
<--- Score

8. What are the costs of reform?
<--- Score

9. Is the solution cost-effective?
<--- Score

10. Are the measurements objective?
<--- Score

11. What has the team done to assure the stability and accuracy of the measurement process?
<--- Score

12. Who should receive measurement reports?
<--- Score

13. What methods are feasible and acceptable to estimate the impact of reforms?
<--- Score

14. Who participated in the data collection for measurements?
<--- Score

15. Are high impact defects defined and identified in the business process?
<--- Score

16. Do you aggressively reward and promote the people who have the biggest impact on creating excellent M2M IoT services/products?
<--- Score

17. Have the types of risks that may impact M2M IoT been identified and analyzed?
<--- Score

18. Is data collected on key measures that were identified?
<--- Score

19. Why do you expend time and effort to implement measurement, for whom?
<--- Score

20. What charts has the team used to display the components of variation in the process?
<--- Score

21. How frequently do you track measures?
<--- Score

22. Is Process Variation Displayed/Communicated?
<--- Score

23. What is an unallowable cost?
<--- Score

24. What potential environmental factors impact the M2M IoT effort?
<--- Score

25. Is a solid data collection plan established that includes measurement systems analysis?
<--- Score

26. What are the key input variables? What are the key process variables? What are the key output variables?
<--- Score

27. Among the M2M IoT product and service cost to be estimated, which is considered hardest to estimate?
<--- Score

28. Is long term and short term variability accounted for?
<--- Score

29. Can you do M2M IoT without complex (expensive) analysis?
<--- Score

30. What do you measure and why?
<--- Score

31. Have you found any 'ground fruit' or 'low-hanging fruit' for immediate remedies to the gap in performance?
<--- Score

32. How will measures be used to manage and adapt?
<--- Score

33. How large is the gap between current performance and the customer-specified (goal) performance?
<--- Score

34. Why do the measurements/indicators matter?
<--- Score

35. How are measurements made?
<--- Score

36. How is the value delivered by M2M IoT being measured?
<--- Score

37. What are the types and number of measures to use?
<--- Score

38. What key measures identified indicate the performance of the business process?
<--- Score

39. Do you effectively measure and reward individual and team performance?
<--- Score

40. Can you measure the return on analysis?
<--- Score

41. How is performance measured?
<--- Score

42. Is there a Performance Baseline?
<--- Score

43. How do you know that any M2M IoT analysis is complete and comprehensive?
<--- Score

44. Does M2M IoT analysis isolate the fundamental causes of problems?
<--- Score

45. How are you going to measure success?
<--- Score

46. Are key measures identified and agreed upon?
<--- Score

47. How frequently do you track M2M IoT measures?
<--- Score

48. What are your key M2M IoT organizational performance measures, including key short and longer-term financial measures?
<--- Score

49. How will your organization measure success?
<--- Score

50. How do you aggregate measures across priorities?
<--- Score

51. Does your organization systematically track and analyze outcomes related for accountability and quality improvement?
<--- Score

52. What is the total cost related to deploying M2M IoT, including any consulting or professional services?
<--- Score

53. How do you control the overall costs of your work processes?
<--- Score

54. How will effects be measured?
<--- Score

55. Is key measure data collection planned and executed, process variation displayed and communicated and performance baselined?
<--- Score

56. What is the right balance of time and resources between investigation, analysis, and discussion and dissemination?
<--- Score

57. What relevant entities could be measured?
<--- Score

58. Are process variation components displayed/ communicated using suitable charts, graphs, plots?
<--- Score

59. Is it possible to estimate the impact of unanticipated complexity such as wrong or failed

assumptions, feedback, etc. on proposed reforms?
<--- Score

60. How is progress measured?
<--- Score

61. How do you do risk analysis of rare, cascading, catastrophic events?
<--- Score

62. How to measure variability?
<--- Score

63. Where is it measured?
<--- Score

64. How do you measure lifecycle phases?
<--- Score

65. Are missed M2M IoT opportunities costing your organization money?
<--- Score

66. Does M2M IoT analysis show the relationships among important M2M IoT factors?
<--- Score

67. Have changes been properly/adequately analyzed for effect?
<--- Score

68. Are losses documented, analyzed, and remedial processes developed to prevent future losses?
<--- Score

69. Will M2M IoT have an impact on current business

continuity, disaster recovery processes and/or infrastructure?

<--- Score

70. Are there measurements based on task performance?

<--- Score

71. What are your key M2M IoT indicators that you will measure, analyze and track?

<--- Score

72. Which measures and indicators matter?

<--- Score

73. Are you taking your company in the direction of better and revenue or cheaper and cost?

<--- Score

74. Which stakeholder characteristics are analyzed?

<--- Score

75. What measurements are being captured?

<--- Score

76. Do staff have the necessary skills to collect, analyze, and report data?

<--- Score

77. Are the units of measure consistent?

<--- Score

78. Was a data collection plan established?

<--- Score

79. How do you measure success?

<--- Score

80. What is measured? Why?
<--- Score

81. How do you stay flexible and focused to recognize larger M2M IoT results?
<--- Score

82. Does the M2M IoT task fit the client's priorities?
<--- Score

83. How do you focus on what is right -not who is right?
<--- Score

84. Have all non-recommended alternatives been analyzed in sufficient detail?
<--- Score

85. What data was collected (past, present, future/ ongoing)?
<--- Score

86. How will you measure your M2M IoT effectiveness?
<--- Score

87. Have the concerns of stakeholders to help identify and define potential barriers been obtained and analyzed?
<--- Score

88. Does M2M IoT systematically track and analyze outcomes for accountability and quality improvement?
<--- Score

89. How do you identify and analyze stakeholders and their interests?
<--- Score

90. What particular quality tools did the team find helpful in establishing measurements?
<--- Score

91. How will you measure success?
<--- Score

92. What are the uncertainties surrounding estimates of impact?
<--- Score

93. How can you measure the performance?
<--- Score

94. Are there any easy-to-implement alternatives to M2M IoT? Sometimes other solutions are available that do not require the cost implications of a full-blown project?
<--- Score

95. What are the agreed upon definitions of the high impact areas, defect(s), unit(s), and opportunities that will figure into the process capability metrics?
<--- Score

96. How can you measure M2M IoT in a systematic way?
<--- Score

Add up total points for this section:
_ _ _ _ _ = Total points for this section

Divided by: _____ (number of
statements answered) = _____
Average score for this section

Transfer your score to the M2M IoT
Index at the beginning of the Self-
Assessment.

CRITERION #4: ANALYZE:

INTENT: Analyze causes, assumptions
and hypotheses.

In my belief, the answer to this
question is clearly defined:

5 Strongly Agree

4 Agree

3 Neutral

2 Disagree

1 Strongly Disagree

1. How often will data be collected for measures?
<--- Score

2. What are your best practices for minimizing M2M
IoT project risk, while demonstrating incremental
value and quick wins throughout the M2M IoT project
lifecycle?
<--- Score

3. Are gaps between current performance and the

goal performance identified?
<--- Score

4. How do you promote understanding that opportunity for improvement is not criticism of the status quo, or the people who created the status quo?
<--- Score

5. What tools were used to generate the list of possible causes?
<--- Score

6. What other jobs or tasks affect the performance of the steps in the M2M IoT process?
<--- Score

7. What conclusions were drawn from the team's data collection and analysis? How did the team reach these conclusions?
<--- Score

8. Have any additional benefits been identified that will result from closing all or most of the gaps?
<--- Score

9. Can you add value to the current M2M IoT decision-making process (largely qualitative) by incorporating uncertainty modeling (more quantitative)?
<--- Score

10. Do your employees have the opportunity to do what they do best everyday?
<--- Score

11. What successful thing are you doing today that may be blinding you to new growth opportunities?

<--- Score

12. Is the gap/opportunity displayed and communicated in financial terms?
<--- Score

13. When conducting a business process reengineering study, what do you look for when trying to identify business processes to change?
<--- Score

14. How do you measure the operational performance of your key work systems and processes, including productivity, cycle time, and other appropriate measures of process effectiveness, efficiency, and innovation?
<--- Score

15. Have the problem and goal statements been updated to reflect the additional knowledge gained from the analyze phase?
<--- Score

16. Do several people in different organizational units assist with the M2M IoT process?
<--- Score

17. What process should you select for improvement?
<--- Score

18. Were any designed experiments used to generate additional insight into the data analysis?
<--- Score

19. Do your leaders quickly bounce back from setbacks?

<--- Score

20. How do you identify specific M2M IoT investment opportunities and emerging trends?
<--- Score

21. A compounding model resolution with available relevant data can often provide insight towards a solution methodology; which M2M IoT models, tools and techniques are necessary?
<--- Score

22. What are your M2M IoT processes?
<--- Score

23. How do your work systems and key work processes relate to and capitalize on your core competencies?
<--- Score

24. An organizationally feasible system request is one that considers the mission, goals and objectives of the organization. Key questions are: is the M2M IoT solution request practical and will it solve a problem or take advantage of an opportunity to achieve company goals?
<--- Score

25. What were the crucial 'moments of truth' on the process map?
<--- Score

26. How do you use M2M IoT data and information to support organizational decision making and innovation?
<--- Score

27. What quality tools were used to get through the analyze phase?
<--- Score

28. Did any value-added analysis or 'lean thinking' take place to identify some of the gaps shown on the 'as is' process map?
<--- Score

29. What are the disruptive M2M IoT technologies that enable your organization to radically change your business processes?
<--- Score

30. Was a detailed process map created to amplify critical steps of the 'as is' business process?
<--- Score

31. What controls do you have in place to protect data?
<--- Score

32. What is the cost of poor quality as supported by the team's analysis?
<--- Score

33. Think about some of the processes you undertake within your organization, which do you own?
<--- Score

34. Record-keeping requirements flow from the records needed as inputs, outputs, controls and for transformation of a M2M IoT process. Are the records needed as inputs to the M2M IoT process available?
<--- Score

35. Think about the functions involved in your M2M IoT project, what processes flow from these functions?
<--- Score

36. How does the organization define, manage, and improve its M2M IoT processes?
<--- Score

37. What are your key performance measures or indicators and in-process measures for the control and improvement of your M2M IoT processes?
<--- Score

38. How was the detailed process map generated, verified, and validated?
<--- Score

39. What other organizational variables, such as reward systems or communication systems, affect the performance of this M2M IoT process?
<--- Score

40. Is the M2M IoT process severely broken such that a re-design is necessary?
<--- Score

41. What tools were used to narrow the list of possible causes?
<--- Score

42. What did the team gain from developing a sub-process map?
<--- Score

43. Is Data and process analysis, root cause analysis

and quantifying the gap/opportunity in place?
<--- Score

44. Is the performance gap determined?
<--- Score

45. What does the data say about the performance of the business process?
<--- Score

46. What are your current levels and trends in key measures or indicators of M2M IoT product and process performance that are important to and directly serve your customers? How do these results compare with the performance of your competitors and other organizations with similar offerings?
<--- Score

47. Where is the data coming from to measure compliance?
<--- Score

48. Is the suppliers process defined and controlled?
<--- Score

49. How do mission and objectives affect the M2M IoT processes of your organization?
<--- Score

50. Was a cause-and-effect diagram used to explore the different types of causes (or sources of variation)?
<--- Score

51. What were the financial benefits resulting from any 'ground fruit or low-hanging fruit' (quick fixes)?
<--- Score

52. Did any additional data need to be collected?
<--- Score

53. Do you, as a leader, bounce back quickly from setbacks?
<--- Score

54. What are your current levels and trends in key M2M IoT measures or indicators of product and process performance that are important to and directly serve your customers?
<--- Score

55. How do you implement and manage your work processes to ensure that they meet design requirements?
<--- Score

56. What are the best opportunities for value improvement?
<--- Score

57. Identify an operational issue in your organization. for example, could a particular task be done more quickly or more efficiently by M2M IoT?
<--- Score

58. Were there any improvement opportunities identified from the process analysis?
<--- Score

59. What are the revised rough estimates of the financial savings/opportunity for M2M IoT improvements?
<--- Score

60. Were Pareto charts (or similar) used to portray the 'heavy hitters' (or key sources of variation)?
<--- Score

61. How is the way you as the leader think and process information affecting your organizational culture?
<--- Score

Add up total points for this section:
_____ = Total points for this section

Divided by: _____ (number of statements answered) = _____
Average score for this section

Transfer your score to the M2M IoT Index at the beginning of the Self-Assessment.

CRITERION #5: IMPROVE:

INTENT: Develop a practical solution. Innovate, establish and test the solution and to measure the results.

In my belief, the answer to this question is clearly defined:

5 Strongly Agree

4 Agree

3 Neutral

2 Disagree

1 Strongly Disagree

1. How does the team improve its work?
<--- Score

2. How do you measure risk?
<--- Score

3. How do you link measurement and risk?
<--- Score

4. Describe the design of the pilot and what tests were conducted, if any?
<--- Score

5. Who will be using the results of the measurement activities?
<--- Score

6. What improvements have been achieved?
<--- Score

7. What is the risk?
<--- Score

8. Was a pilot designed for the proposed solution(s)?
<--- Score

9. How do you measure improved M2M IoT service perception, and satisfaction?
<--- Score

10. Why improve in the first place?
<--- Score

11. Are possible solutions generated and tested?
<--- Score

12. What are the implications of the one critical M2M IoT decision 10 minutes, 10 months, and 10 years from now?
<--- Score

13. Do those selected for the M2M IoT team have a good general understanding of what M2M IoT is all about?
<--- Score

14. Is supporting M2M IoT documentation required?
<--- Score

15. How significant is the improvement in the eyes of the end user?
<--- Score

16. What tools were most useful during the improve phase?
<--- Score

17. What lessons, if any, from a pilot were incorporated into the design of the full-scale solution?
<--- Score

18. What should a proof of concept or pilot accomplish?
<--- Score

19. Is the measure of success for M2M IoT understandable to a variety of people?
<--- Score

20. What is the magnitude of the improvements?
<--- Score

21. How can skill-level changes improve M2M IoT?
<--- Score

22. How will you measure the results?
<--- Score

23. What communications are necessary to support the implementation of the solution?
<--- Score

24. Is the implementation plan designed?
<--- Score

25. What is the M2M IoT's sustainability risk?
<--- Score

26. How will you know that you have improved?
<--- Score

27. How will the organization know that the solution worked?
<--- Score

28. How will the team or the process owner(s) monitor the implementation plan to see that it is working as intended?
<--- Score

29. What tools do you use once you have decided on a M2M IoT strategy and more importantly how do you choose?
<--- Score

30. Explorations of the frontiers of M2M IoT will help you build influence, improve M2M IoT, optimize decision making, and sustain change, what is your approach?
<--- Score

31. Does the goal represent a desired result that can be measured?
<--- Score

32. Are there any constraints (technical, political, cultural, or otherwise) that would inhibit certain

solutions?
<--- Score

33. How do you keep improving M2M IoT?
<--- Score

34. What actually has to improve and by how much?
<--- Score

35. Are improved process ('should be') maps modified based on pilot data and analysis?
<--- Score

36. What resources are required for the improvement efforts?
<--- Score

37. What do you want to improve?
<--- Score

38. Is there a cost/benefit analysis of optimal solution(s)?
<--- Score

39. What error proofing will be done to address some of the discrepancies observed in the 'as is' process?
<--- Score

40. For decision problems, how do you develop a decision statement?
<--- Score

41. What tools were used to tap into the creativity and encourage 'outside the box' thinking?
<--- Score

42. If you could go back in time five years, what decision would you make differently? What is your best guess as to what decision you're making today you might regret five years from now?
<--- Score

43. Are the best solutions selected?
<--- Score

44. What are your current levels and trends in key measures or indicators of workforce and leader development?
<--- Score

45. What tools were used to evaluate the potential solutions?
<--- Score

46. Do you combine technical expertise with business knowledge and M2M IoT Key topics include lifecycles, development approaches, requirements and how to make a business case?
<--- Score

47. What to do with the results or outcomes of measurements?
<--- Score

48. How will you know when its improved?
<--- Score

49. What were the underlying assumptions on the cost-benefit analysis?
<--- Score

50. How do you improve M2M IoT service perception,

and satisfaction?
<--- Score

51. Who will be responsible for making the decisions to include or exclude requested changes once M2M IoT is underway?
<--- Score

52. How do you measure progress and evaluate training effectiveness?
<--- Score

53. Risk events: what are the things that could go wrong?
<--- Score

54. How do you manage and improve your M2M IoT work systems to deliver customer value and achieve organizational success and sustainability?
<--- Score

55. What can you do to improve?
<--- Score

56. Is there a high likelihood that any recommendations will achieve their intended results?
<--- Score

57. How will you know that a change is an improvement?
<--- Score

58. Are you assessing M2M IoT and risk?
<--- Score

59. What is the team's contingency plan for potential

problems occurring in implementation?
<--- Score

60. Who controls key decisions that will be made?
<--- Score

61. Do you cover the five essential competencies: Communication, Collaboration,Innovation, Adaptability, and Leadership that improve an organization's ability to leverage the new M2M IoT in a volatile global economy?
<--- Score

62. What is the implementation plan?
<--- Score

63. How do you improve productivity?
<--- Score

64. How do you go about comparing M2M IoT approaches/solutions?
<--- Score

65. Can the solution be designed and implemented within an acceptable time period?
<--- Score

66. At what point will vulnerability assessments be performed once M2M IoT is put into production (e.g., ongoing Risk Management after implementation)?
<--- Score

67. Who are the people involved in developing and implementing M2M IoT?
<--- Score

68. Is there a small-scale pilot for proposed improvement(s)? What conclusions were drawn from the outcomes of a pilot?
<--- Score

69. What is M2M IoT's impact on utilizing the best solution(s)?
<--- Score

70. Is the optimal solution selected based on testing and analysis?
<--- Score

71. Is the solution technically practical?
<--- Score

72. How did the team generate the list of possible solutions?
<--- Score

73. In the past few months, what is the smallest change you have made that has had the biggest positive result? What was it about that small change that produced the large return?
<--- Score

74. Is pilot data collected and analyzed?
<--- Score

75. What does the 'should be' process map/design look like?
<--- Score

76. What went well, what should change, what can improve?
<--- Score

77. To what extent does management recognize M2M IoT as a tool to increase the results?
<--- Score

78. What attendant changes will need to be made to ensure that the solution is successful?
<--- Score

79. Were any criteria developed to assist the team in testing and evaluating potential solutions?
<--- Score

80. How can you improve M2M IoT?
<--- Score

81. Who controls the risk?
<--- Score

82. What needs improvement? Why?
<--- Score

83. Risk factors: what are the characteristics of M2M IoT that make it risky?
<--- Score

84. Is a contingency plan established?
<--- Score

85. For estimation problems, how do you develop an estimation statement?
<--- Score

86. How do you improve your likelihood of success ?
<--- Score

87. Is a solution implementation plan established, including schedule/work breakdown structure, resources, risk management plan, cost/budget, and control plan?
<--- Score

88. Who will be responsible for documenting the M2M IoT requirements in detail?
<--- Score

89. How can you improve performance?
<--- Score

90. How do you decide how much to remunerate an employee?
<--- Score

91. Are new and improved process ('should be') maps developed?
<--- Score

92. How do the M2M IoT results compare with the performance of your competitors and other organizations with similar offerings?
<--- Score

93. How does the solution remove the key sources of issues discovered in the analyze phase?
<--- Score

Add up total points for this section:
_ _ _ _ _ = Total points for this section

Divided by: _ _ _ _ _ _ (number of statements answered) = _ _ _ _ _ _
Average score for this section

Transfer your score to the M2M IoT
Index at the beginning of the Self-
Assessment.

CRITERION #6: CONTROL:

INTENT: Implement the practical solution. Maintain the performance and correct possible complications.

In my belief, the answer to this question is clearly defined:

5 Strongly Agree

4 Agree

3 Neutral

2 Disagree

1 Strongly Disagree

1. Are the planned controls in place?
<--- Score

2. Is there documentation that will support the successful operation of the improvement?
<--- Score

3. Are operating procedures consistent?
<--- Score

4. Will existing staff require re-training, for example, to learn new business processes?
<--- Score

5. Have new or revised work instructions resulted?
<--- Score

6. Who has control over resources?
<--- Score

7. Is a response plan established and deployed?
<--- Score

8. What can you control?
<--- Score

9. Are documented procedures clear and easy to follow for the operators?
<--- Score

10. How do controls support value?
<--- Score

11. Is there a recommended audit plan for routine surveillance inspections of M2M IoT's gains?
<--- Score

12. Who controls critical resources?
<--- Score

13. Implementation Planning- is a pilot needed to test the changes before a full roll out occurs?
<--- Score

14. What new information will be needed to adjust

technology scenarios as time advances?
<--- Score

15. What should you measure to verify efficiency gains?
<--- Score

16. Is there a documented and implemented monitoring plan?
<--- Score

17. Are controls in place and consistently applied?
<--- Score

18. Do you monitor the effectiveness of your M2M IoT activities?
<--- Score

19. How likely is the current M2M IoT plan to come in on schedule or on budget?
<--- Score

20. Does a troubleshooting guide exist or is it needed?
<--- Score

21. Is there a control plan in place for sustaining improvements (short and long-term)?
<--- Score

22. What key inputs and outputs are being measured on an ongoing basis?
<--- Score

23. Is there a transfer of ownership and knowledge to process owner and process team tasked with the responsibilities.

<--- Score

24. Against what alternative is success being measured?
<--- Score

25. Do you monitor the M2M IoT decisions made and fine tune them as they evolve?
<--- Score

26. Who will be in control?
<--- Score

27. What are you attempting to measure/monitor?
<--- Score

28. How will the day-to-day responsibilities for monitoring and continual improvement be transferred from the improvement team to the process owner?
<--- Score

29. What do you stand for--and what are you against?
<--- Score

30. What is the control/monitoring plan?
<--- Score

31. How is change control managed?
<--- Score

32. In the case of a M2M IoT project, the criteria for the audit derive from implementation objectives. an audit of a M2M IoT project involves assessing whether the recommendations outlined for implementation have been met. Can you track that any M2M IoT project is

implemented as planned, and is it working?
<--- Score

33. Does M2M IoT appropriately measure and monitor risk?
<--- Score

34. What do you measure to verify effectiveness gains?
<--- Score

35. Is an adjustment or replacement essential?
<--- Score

36. Are there documented procedures?
<--- Score

37. How might the organization capture best practices and lessons learned so as to leverage improvements across the business?
<--- Score

38. How do your controls stack up?
<--- Score

39. How do you establish and deploy modified action plans if circumstances require a shift in plans and rapid execution of new plans?
<--- Score

40. How do you select, collect, align, and integrate M2M IoT data and information for tracking daily operations and overall organizational performance, including progress relative to strategic objectives and action plans?
<--- Score

41. How will new or emerging customer needs/requirements be checked/communicated to orient the process toward meeting the new specifications and continually reducing variation?
<--- Score

42. What other areas of the organization might benefit from the M2M IoT team's improvements, knowledge, and learning?
<--- Score

43. What quality tools were useful in the control phase?
<--- Score

44. Does the response plan contain a definite closed loop continual improvement scheme (e.g., plan-do-check-act)?
<--- Score

45. What are the critical parameters to watch?
<--- Score

46. Do the M2M IoT decisions you make today help people and the planet tomorrow?
<--- Score

47. Who is the M2M IoT process owner?
<--- Score

48. Are new process steps, standards, and documentation ingrained into normal operations?
<--- Score

49. What is your theory of human motivation, and

how does your compensation plan fit with that view?
<--- Score

50. Are you measuring, monitoring and predicting M2M IoT activities to optimize operations and profitability, and enhancing outcomes?
<--- Score

51. What are your results for key measures or indicators of the accomplishment of your M2M IoT strategy and action plans, including building and strengthening core competencies?
<--- Score

52. Will any special training be provided for results interpretation?
<--- Score

53. How will the process owner and team be able to hold the gains?
<--- Score

54. Are the planned controls working?
<--- Score

55. What are the key elements of your M2M IoT performance improvement system, including your evaluation, organizational learning, and innovation processes?
<--- Score

56. What are the known security controls?
<--- Score

57. How will input, process, and output variables be checked to detect for sub-optimal conditions?

<--- Score

58. How do you encourage people to take control and responsibility?
<--- Score

59. You may have created your quality measures at a time when you lacked resources, technology wasn't up to the required standard, or low service levels were the industry norm. Have those circumstances changed?
<--- Score

60. What should the next improvement project be that is related to M2M IoT?
<--- Score

61. Are suggested corrective/restorative actions indicated on the response plan for known causes to problems that might surface?
<--- Score

62. Is there a M2M IoT Communication plan covering who needs to get what information when?
<--- Score

63. Who sets the M2M IoT standards?
<--- Score

64. When are adjustments required?
<--- Score

65. What is the recommended frequency of auditing?
<--- Score

66. How will the process owner verify improvement in

present and future sigma levels, process capabilities?
<--- Score

67. Is knowledge gained on process shared and institutionalized?
<--- Score

68. Is a response plan in place for when the input, process, or output measures indicate an 'out-of-control' condition?
<--- Score

69. What is the best design framework for M2M IoT organization now that, in a post industrial-age if the top-down, command and control model is no longer relevant?
<--- Score

70. Has the improved process and its steps been standardized?
<--- Score

71. What other systems, operations, processes, and infrastructures (hiring practices, staffing, training, incentives/rewards, metrics/dashboards/scorecards, etc.) need updates, additions, changes, or deletions in order to facilitate knowledge transfer and improvements?
<--- Score

72. Is there a standardized process?
<--- Score

73. Does the M2M IoT performance meet the customer's requirements?
<--- Score

74. Do the decisions you make today help people and the planet tomorrow?
<--- Score

75. Where do ideas that reach policy makers and planners as proposals for M2M IoT strengthening and reform actually originate?
<--- Score

76. Is reporting being used or needed?
<--- Score

77. How will report readings be checked to effectively monitor performance?
<--- Score

78. Is new knowledge gained imbedded in the response plan?
<--- Score

79. How can you best use all of your knowledge repositories to enhance learning and sharing?
<--- Score

80. Are pertinent alerts monitored, analyzed and distributed to appropriate personnel?
<--- Score

81. Does job training on the documented procedures need to be part of the process team's education and training?
<--- Score

Add up total points for this section:
_ _ _ _ _ = Total points for this section

Divided by: _ _ _ _ _ _ (number of
statements answered) = _ _ _ _ _ _
Average score for this section

Transfer your score to the M2M IoT
Index at the beginning of the Self-
Assessment.

CRITERION #7: SUSTAIN:

1. In retrospect, of the projects that you pulled the plug on, what percent do you wish had been allowed to keep going, and what percent do you wish had ended earlier?
<--- Score

2. How do you govern and fulfill your societal responsibilities?
<--- Score

3. How can you become more high-tech but still be

high touch?
<--- Score

4. What happens when a new employee joins the organization?
<--- Score

5. What knowledge, skills and characteristics mark a good M2M IoT project manager?
<--- Score

6. Who will determine interim and final deadlines?
<--- Score

7. What are strategies for increasing support and reducing opposition?
<--- Score

8. What is something you believe that nearly no one agrees with you on?
<--- Score

9. Which models, tools and techniques are necessary?
<--- Score

10. Do you think you know, or do you know you know ?
<--- Score

11. What are the usability implications of M2M IoT actions?
<--- Score

12. Would you rather sell to knowledgeable and informed customers or to uninformed customers?
<--- Score

13. What role does communication play in the success or failure of a M2M IoT project?
<--- Score

14. What is the kind of project structure that would be appropriate for your M2M IoT project, should it be formal and complex, or can it be less formal and relatively simple?
<--- Score

15. What is your BATNA (best alternative to a negotiated agreement)?
<--- Score

16. Who is responsible for ensuring appropriate resources (time, people and money) are allocated to M2M IoT?
<--- Score

17. What potential megatrends could make your business model obsolete?
<--- Score

18. How do customers see your organization?
<--- Score

19. Who are the key stakeholders?
<--- Score

20. What are the success criteria that will indicate that M2M IoT objectives have been met and the benefits delivered?
<--- Score

21. What may be the consequences for the

performance of an organization if all stakeholders are not consulted regarding M2M IoT?

<--- Score

22. How are you doing compared to your industry?

<--- Score

23. What would you recommend your friend do if he/she were facing this dilemma?

<--- Score

24. How do you ensure that implementations of M2M IoT products are done in a way that ensures safety?

<--- Score

25. What one word do you want to own in the minds of your customers, employees, and partners?

<--- Score

26. Who else should you help?

<--- Score

27. What is your M2M IoT strategy?

<--- Score

28. What would have to be true for the option on the table to be the best possible choice?

<--- Score

29. What is your formula for success in M2M IoT ?

<--- Score

30. What is the purpose of M2M IoT in relation to the mission?

<--- Score

31. Is there any existing M2M IoT governance structure?
<--- Score

32. What are the key enablers to make this M2M IoT move?
<--- Score

33. What is it like to work for you?
<--- Score

34. How much contingency will be available in the budget?
<--- Score

35. Which functions and people interact with the supplier and or customer?
<--- Score

36. Who have you, as a company, historically been when you've been at your best?
<--- Score

37. What are the essentials of internal M2M IoT management?
<--- Score

38. What will be the consequences to the stakeholder (financial, reputation etc) if M2M IoT does not go ahead or fails to deliver the objectives?
<--- Score

39. What are the potential basics of M2M IoT fraud?
<--- Score

40. How do you engage the workforce, in addition to

satisfying them?
<--- Score

41. Why do and why don't your customers like your organization?
<--- Score

42. Who is the main stakeholder, with ultimate responsibility for driving M2M IoT forward?
<--- Score

43. What are specific M2M IoT rules to follow?
<--- Score

44. What kind of crime could a potential new hire have committed that would not only not disqualify him/her from being hired by your organization, but would actually indicate that he/she might be a particularly good fit?
<--- Score

45. Are there any disadvantages to implementing M2M IoT? There might be some that are less obvious?
<--- Score

46. Where can you break convention?
<--- Score

47. How long will it take to change?
<--- Score

48. Why is M2M IoT important for you now?
<--- Score

49. How do you listen to customers to obtain actionable information?

<--- Score

50. How do you determine the key elements that affect M2M IoT workforce satisfaction, how are these elements determined for different workforce groups and segments?
<--- Score

51. Do you have the right capabilities and capacities?
<--- Score

52. How do you make it meaningful in connecting M2M IoT with what users do day-to-day?
<--- Score

53. What are the barriers to increased M2M IoT production?
<--- Score

54. Who is on the team?
<--- Score

55. How do you cross-sell and up-sell your M2M IoT success?
<--- Score

56. Who do you think the world wants your organization to be?
<--- Score

57. If your company went out of business tomorrow, would anyone who doesn't get a paycheck here care?
<--- Score

58. How can you incorporate support to ensure safe and effective use of M2M IoT into the services that

you provide?
<--- Score

59. What M2M IoT skills are most important?
<--- Score

60. How do you provide a safe environment
-physically and emotionally?
<--- Score

61. Are the assumptions believable and achievable?
<--- Score

62. Who, on the executive team or the board, has
spoken to a customer recently?
<--- Score

63. What is your competitive advantage?
<--- Score

64. Do you have the right people on the bus?
<--- Score

65. What is the funding source for this project?
<--- Score

66. How do you track customer value, profitability
or financial return, organizational success, and
sustainability?
<--- Score

67. If you got fired and a new hire took your place,
what would she do different?
<--- Score

68. What are current M2M IoT paradigms?

<--- Score

69. How do you foster the skills, knowledge, talents, attributes, and characteristics you want to have?
<--- Score

70. If you were responsible for initiating and implementing major changes in your organization, what steps might you take to ensure acceptance of those changes?
<--- Score

71. What business benefits will M2M IoT goals deliver if achieved?
<--- Score

72. What are your most important goals for the strategic M2M IoT objectives?
<--- Score

73. Did your employees make progress today?
<--- Score

74. What management system can you use to leverage the M2M IoT experience, ideas, and concerns of the people closest to the work to be done?
<--- Score

75. Is a M2M IoT team work effort in place?
<--- Score

76. How is business? Why?
<--- Score

77. Operational - will it work?
<--- Score

78. How do you deal with M2M IoT changes?
<--- Score

79. Do you have an implicit bias for capital investments over people investments?
<--- Score

80. Is your strategy driving your strategy? Or is the way in which you allocate resources driving your strategy?
<--- Score

81. How do senior leaders actions reflect a commitment to the organizations M2M IoT values?
<--- Score

82. How can you negotiate M2M IoT successfully with a stubborn boss, an irate client, or a deceitful coworker?
<--- Score

83. Are you making progress, and are you making progress as M2M IoT leaders?
<--- Score

84. What should you stop doing?
<--- Score

85. Are you using a design thinking approach and integrating Innovation, M2M IoT Experience, and Brand Value?
<--- Score

86. Are new benefits received and understood?
<--- Score

87. What new services of functionality will be implemented next with M2M IoT ?
<--- Score

88. How much does M2M IoT help?
<--- Score

89. If you do not follow, then how to lead?
<--- Score

90. What are the business goals M2M IoT is aiming to achieve?
<--- Score

91. How will you insure seamless interoperability of M2M IoT moving forward?
<--- Score

92. What happens at your organization when people fail?
<--- Score

93. To whom do you add value?
<--- Score

94. Who uses your product in ways you never expected?
<--- Score

95. Are you failing differently each time?
<--- Score

96. Whose voice (department, ethnic group, women, older workers, etc) might you have missed hearing from in your company, and how might you amplify

this voice to create positive momentum for your business?
<--- Score

97. How do you maintain M2M IoT's Integrity?
<--- Score

98. Can the schedule be done in the given time?
<--- Score

99. What did you miss in the interview for the worst hire you ever made?
<--- Score

100. Do you see more potential in people than they do in themselves?
<--- Score

101. Ask yourself: how would you do this work if you only had one staff member to do it?
<--- Score

102. How do you proactively clarify deliverables and M2M IoT quality expectations?
<--- Score

103. What are the top 3 things at the forefront of your M2M IoT agendas for the next 3 years?
<--- Score

104. What do we do when new problems arise?
<--- Score

105. How do you manage M2M IoT Knowledge Management (KM)?
<--- Score

106. If you had to leave your organization for a year and the only communication you could have with employees/colleagues was a single paragraph, what would you write?
<--- Score

107. Do you know what you are doing? And who do you call if you don't?
<--- Score

108. Have benefits been optimized with all key stakeholders?
<--- Score

109. Were lessons learned captured and communicated?
<--- Score

110. Do M2M IoT rules make a reasonable demand on a users capabilities?
<--- Score

111. Why should you adopt a M2M IoT framework?
<--- Score

112. What are the long-term M2M IoT goals?
<--- Score

113. Who will be responsible for deciding whether M2M IoT goes ahead or not after the initial investigations?
<--- Score

114. Are you satisfied with your current role? If not, what is missing from it?

<--- Score

115. Is the M2M IoT organization completing tasks effectively and efficiently?
<--- Score

116. How do you foster innovation?
<--- Score

117. In the past year, what have you done (or could you have done) to increase the accurate perception of your company/brand as ethical and honest?
<--- Score

118. Marketing budgets are tighter, consumers are more skeptical, and social media has changed forever the way we talk about M2M IoT. How do you gain traction?
<--- Score

119. Will there be any necessary staff changes (redundancies or new hires)?
<--- Score

120. What are the short and long-term M2M IoT goals?
<--- Score

121. Is there any reason to believe the opposite of my current belief?
<--- Score

122. What current systems have to be understood and/or changed?
<--- Score

123. Do you say no to customers for no reason?

<--- Score

124. If your customer were your grandmother, would you tell her to buy what you're selling?
<--- Score

125. Are the criteria for selecting recommendations stated?
<--- Score

126. How will you motivate the stakeholders with the least vested interest?
<--- Score

127. Among your stronger employees, how many see themselves at the company in three years? How many would leave for a 10 percent raise from another company?
<--- Score

128. How do you know if you are successful?
<--- Score

129. What was the last experiment you ran?
<--- Score

130. How does M2M IoT integrate with other business initiatives?
<--- Score

131. Will it be accepted by users?
<--- Score

132. What trouble can you get into?
<--- Score

133. Think of your M2M IoT project, what are the main functions?
<--- Score

134. What will drive M2M IoT change?
<--- Score

135. When information truly is ubiquitous, when reach and connectivity are completely global, when computing resources are infinite, and when a whole new set of impossibilities are not only possible, but happening, what will that do to your business?
<--- Score

136. Why is it important to have senior management support for a M2M IoT project?
<--- Score

137. Is maximizing M2M IoT protection the same as minimizing M2M IoT loss?
<--- Score

138. If no one would ever find out about your accomplishments, how would you lead differently?
<--- Score

139. What are the rules and assumptions your industry operates under? What if the opposite were true?
<--- Score

140. Who is responsible for errors?
<--- Score

141. Which individuals, teams or departments will be involved in M2M IoT?
<--- Score

142. How do senior leaders deploy your organizations vision and values through your leadership system, to the workforce, to key suppliers and partners, and to customers and other stakeholders, as appropriate?
<--- Score

143. What is the estimated value of the project?
<--- Score

144. How do you keep records, of what?
<--- Score

145. Has implementation been effective in reaching specified objectives so far?
<--- Score

146. What is the source of the strategies for M2M IoT strengthening and reform?
<--- Score

147. What is effective M2M IoT?
<--- Score

148. Can you maintain your growth without detracting from the factors that have contributed to your success?
<--- Score

149. How will you ensure you get what you expected?
<--- Score

150. How do you create buy-in?
<--- Score

151. Are you relevant? Will you be relevant five years

from now? Ten?

<--- Score

152. Who do we want your customers to become?

<--- Score

153. How do you go about securing M2M IoT?

<--- Score

154. Are you paying enough attention to the partners your company depends on to succeed?

<--- Score

155. How will you know that the M2M IoT project has been successful?

<--- Score

156. What is your question? Why?

<--- Score

157. In a project to restructure M2M IoT outcomes, which stakeholders would you involve?

<--- Score

158. Are you / should you be revolutionary or evolutionary?

<--- Score

159. Is M2M IoT realistic, or are you setting yourself up for failure?

<--- Score

160. Why should people listen to you?

<--- Score

161. What is the overall business strategy?

<--- Score

162. Is it economical; do you have the time and money?
<--- Score

163. How can you become the company that would put you out of business?
<--- Score

164. Instead of going to current contacts for new ideas, what if you reconnected with dormant contacts--the people you used to know? If you were going reactivate a dormant tie, who would it be?
<--- Score

165. What are internal and external M2M IoT relations?
<--- Score

166. How do you assess the M2M IoT pitfalls that are inherent in implementing it?
<--- Score

167. What have you done to protect your business from competitive encroachment?
<--- Score

168. What threat is M2M IoT addressing?
<--- Score

169. What happens if you do not have enough funding?
<--- Score

170. What stupid rule would you most like to kill?
<--- Score

171. What sources do you use to gather information for a M2M IoT study?
<--- Score

172. Do you have enough freaky customers in your portfolio pushing you to the limit day in and day out?
<--- Score

173. Is M2M IoT dependent on the successful delivery of a current project?
<--- Score

174. Are you changing as fast as the world around you?
<--- Score

175. What are you trying to prove to yourself, and how might it be hijacking your life and business success?
<--- Score

176. What does your signature ensure?
<--- Score

177. Why not do M2M IoT?
<--- Score

178. What information is critical to your organization that your executives are ignoring?
<--- Score

179. Whom among your colleagues do you trust, and for what?
<--- Score

180. Political -is anyone trying to undermine this

project?
<--- Score

181. Which M2M IoT goals are the most important?
<--- Score

182. How likely is it that a customer would recommend your company to a friend or colleague?
<--- Score

183. Do you have past M2M IoT successes?
<--- Score

184. What trophy do you want on your mantle?
<--- Score

185. Who will provide the final approval of M2M IoT deliverables?
<--- Score

186. What are the challenges?
<--- Score

187. Have new benefits been realized?
<--- Score

188. How do you accomplish your long range M2M IoT goals?
<--- Score

189. What is an unauthorized commitment?
<--- Score

190. How do you keep the momentum going?
<--- Score

191. What is a feasible sequencing of reform initiatives over time?
<--- Score

192. If you weren't already in this business, would you enter it today? And if not, what are you going to do about it?
<--- Score

193. How do you lead with M2M IoT in mind?
<--- Score

194. How important is M2M IoT to the user organizations mission?
<--- Score

195. Who will manage the integration of tools?
<--- Score

196. Is the impact that M2M IoT has shown?
<--- Score

197. If there were zero limitations, what would you do differently?
<--- Score

198. How do you stay inspired?
<--- Score

199. What is the craziest thing you can do?
<--- Score

200. Who do you want your customers to become?
<--- Score

201. What counts that you are not counting?

<--- Score

202. What are you challenging?
<--- Score

203. What are the gaps in your knowledge and experience?
<--- Score

204. Who are four people whose careers you have enhanced?
<--- Score

205. Are assumptions made in M2M IoT stated explicitly?
<--- Score

206. At what moment would you think; Will I get fired?
<--- Score

207. Who is responsible for M2M IoT?
<--- Score

208. If you had to rebuild your organization without any traditional competitive advantages (i.e., no killer a technology, promising research, innovative product/service delivery model, etc.), how would your people have to approach their work and collaborate together in order to create the necessary conditions for success?
<--- Score

209. What is the range of capabilities?
<--- Score

Add up total points for this section:

_____ = Total points for this section

Divided by: _____ (number of statements answered) = _____ Average score for this section

Transfer your score to the M2M IoT Index at the beginning of the Self-Assessment.

M2M IoT and Managing Projects, Criteria for Project Managers:

1.0 Initiating Process Group: M2M IoT

1. Who is involved in each phase?

2. How well defined and documented were the M2M IoT project management processes you chose to use?

3. Were resources available as planned?

4. How Will You Do It?

5. Are you certain deliverables are properly completed and meet quality standards?

6. Are stakeholders properly informed about the status of the M2M IoT project?

7. How will it affect me?

8. What is the stake of others in your M2M IoT project?

9. What are the short and long term implications?

10. Do you know if the M2M IoT project requires outside equipment or vendor resources?

11. What are the pressing issues of the hour?

12. At which stage, in a typical M2M IoT project do stake holders have maximum influence?

13. What are the constraints?

14. Just how important is your work to the overall success of the M2M IoT project?

15. What do they need to know about the M2M IoT project?

16. How is each deliverable reviewed, verified, and validated?

17. Did the M2M IoT project team have the right skills?

18. For technology M2M IoT projects only: Are all production support stakeholders (Business unit, technical support, & user) prepared for implementation with appropriate contingency plans?

19. What areas were overlooked on this M2M IoT project?

20. Measurable - Are the targets measurable?

1.1 Project Charter: M2M IoT

21. What are you trying to accomplish?

22. Environmental Stewardship and Sustainability Considerations: What is the process that will be used to ensure compliance with the Environmental Stewardship Policy?

23. What changes can you make to improve?

24. Whose input and support will this M2M IoT project require?

25. Pop Quiz – Which are the same inputs as in the M2M IoT project Charter?

26. What metrics could you look at?

27. Is time of the essence?

28. Must Have?

29. What material?

30. Customer Benefits: What customer requirements does this M2M IoT project address?

31. What outcome, in measureable terms, are you hoping to accomplish?

32. Who is the M2M IoT project Manager?

33. Rough time estimate 2 months or 2 yrs?

34. Why the Improvements?

35. Who Manages Integration?

36. How Do you Manage Integration?

37. What are the deliverables?

38. Did your M2M IoT project ask for this?

39. Name and describe the elements that deal with providing the detail?

40. Fit with other Products Compliments – Cannibalizes?

1.2 Stakeholder Register: M2M IoT

41. Who are the stakeholders?

42. How will Reports Be Created?

43. What opportunities exist to provide communications?

44. How Big is the Gap?

45. How should employers make their voices heard?

46. How much influence do they have on the M2M IoT project?

47. Is Your Organization Ready for Change?

48. Who wants to talk about Security?

49. What & Why?

50. What is the power of the stakeholder?

51. Who is Managing Stakeholder Engagement?

52. What are the major M2M IoT project milestones requiring communications or providing communications opportunities?

1.3 Stakeholder Analysis Matrix: M2M IoT

53. What coalitions might build around the issues being tackled?

54. Volumes, production, economies?

55. Are there people whose voices or interests in the issue may not be heard?

56. Contributions to policy and practice?

57. Who has not been involved up to now but should have been?

58. Identify the stakeholders levels most frequently used –or at least sought– in your M2M IoT projects and for which purpose?

59. What makes a person a stakeholder?

60. What is their relationship with the M2M IoT project?

61. Which resources are required?

62. How to involve media?

63. Who will be affected by the M2M IoT project?

64. Reputation, presence and reach?

65. Disadvantages of proposition?

66. What is the organizations competitors doing?

67. Financial reserves, likely returns?

68. Why do you need to manage M2M IoT project Risk?

69. Where are the good opportunities facing our organizations development?

70. What unique or lowest-cost resources does the M2M IoT project have access to?

71. What do people from other organizations see as our organizations weaknesses?

72. Partnerships, agencies, distribution?

2.0 Planning Process Group: M2M IoT

73. How well do the team follow the chosen processes?

74. Professionals want to know what is expected from them; what are the deliverables?

75. What do they need to know about the M2M IoT project?

76. How well will the chosen processes produce the expected results?

77. How will users learn how to use the deliverables?

78. What type of estimation method are you using?

79. Will the products created live up to the necessary quality?

80. What Business Situation Is Being Addressed?

81. Just how important is your work to the overall success of the M2M IoT project?

82. To what extent and in what ways are the M2M IoT project contributing to progress towards organizational reform?

83. The M2M IoT project Charter is created in which M2M IoT project management process group?

84. To what extent are the participating departments

coordinating with each other?

85. Did you read it correctly?

86. What is the critical path for this M2M IoT project, and what is the duration of the critical path?

87. What is a Software Development Life Cycle (SDLC)?

88. Is the identification of the problems, inequalities and gaps, with their respective causes, clear in the M2M IoT project?

89. In what way has the program contributed towards the issue culture and development included on the public agenda?

90. Is the M2M IoT project supported by national and/or local organizations?

91. If task X starts two days late, what is the effect on the M2M IoT project end date?

2.1 Project Management Plan: M2M IoT

92. Did the planning effort collaborate to develop solutions that integrate expertise, policies, programs, and M2M IoT projects across entities?

93. What if, for example, the positive direction and vision of the organization causes expected trends to change resulting in greater need than expected?

94. Why Change?

95. When is the M2M IoT project management plan created?

96. If the M2M IoT project is complex or scope is specialized, do you have appropriate and/or qualified staff available to perform the tasks?

97. What are the assumptions?

98. Will you add a schedule and diagram?

99. Is the engineering content at a feasibility level-of-detail, and is it sufficiently complete, to provide an adequate basis for the baseline cost estimate?

100. Do the proposed changes from the M2M IoT project include any significant risks to safety?

101. Where does all this information come from?

102. Are comparable cost estimates used for comparing, screening and selecting alternative plans, and has a reasonable cost estimate been developed for the recommended plan?

103. Who is the M2M IoT project Manager?

104. Development trends and opportunities. What if the positive direction and vision of the organization causes expected trends to change?

105. What Went Right?

106. What goes into your M2M IoT project Charter?

107. Is the budget realistic?

108. What is M2M IoT project Scope Management?

109. What Went Wrong?

110. What is the justification?

2.2 Scope Management Plan: M2M IoT

111. Has the M2M IoT project manager been identified?

112. How do you know when you are finished?

113. What should you drop in order to add something new?

114. Are the proposed M2M IoT project purposes different than the previously authorized M2M IoT project?

115. Are changes in deliverable commitments agreed to by all affected groups & individuals?

116. Have the procedures for identifying variances from estimates & adjusting the detailed work program been followed?

117. What Does the Critical Path Really Mean?

118. Assess the expected stability of the scope of this M2M IoT project how likely is it to change, how frequently, and by how much?

119. Has the schedule been baselined?

120. Have adequate resources been provided by management to ensure M2M IoT project success?

121. What are the risks that could significantly affect the budget of the M2M IoT project?

122. Quality Standards - Are controls in place to ensure that the work was not only completed but also completed to meet specific standards?

123. Is the quality assurance team identified?

124. Is documentation created for communication with the suppliers and Vendors?

125. Is there a Steering Committee in place?

126. What do you need to do to accomplish the goal or goals?

127. What work performance data will be captured?

128. Does the M2M IoT project team have the skills necessary to successfully complete current M2M IoT project(s) and support the application?

129. What is the unique product, service or result?

130. Are assumptions being identified, recorded, analyzed, qualified and closed?

2.3 Requirements Management Plan: M2M IoT

131. Do you really need to write this document at all?

132. Have stakeholders been instructed in the Change Control process?

133. What are you trying to do?

134. Did you avoid subjective, flowery or non-specific statements?

135. What performance metrics will be used?

136. Do you have an agreed upon process for alerting the M2M IoT project Manager if a request for change in requirements leads to a product scope change?

137. What information regarding the M2M IoT project requirements will be reported?

138. Are actual resources expenditures versus planned expenditures acceptable?

139. How will you develop the schedule of requirements activities?

140. Is there formal agreement on who has authority to approve a change in requirements?

141. Why Manage Requirements?

142. Will you use tracing to help understand the impact of a change in requirements?

143. How will unresolved questions be handled once approval has been obtained?

144. Who came up with this requirement?

145. What cost metrics will be used?

146. Will the product release be stable and mature enough to be deployed in the user community?

147. What is the earliest finish date for this M2M IoT project if it is scheduled to start on ...?

148. If it exists, where is it housed?

149. Will the contractors involved take full responsibility?

150. How will bidders price evaluations be done, by deliverables, phases, or in a big bang?

2.4 Requirements Documentation: M2M IoT

151. How does what is being described meet the business need?

152. How will the proposed M2M IoT project help?

153. What if the system wasn t implemented?

154. Are there any requirements conflicts?

155. How much testing do you need to do to prove that my system is safe?

156. What are the potential disadvantages/ advantages?

157. Where are business rules being captured?

158. Can the requirement be changed without a large impact on other requirements?

159. What is Effective documentation?

160. How do you get the user to tell you what they want?

161. Who is interacting with the system?

162. If applicable; are there issues linked with the fact that this is an offshore M2M IoT project?

163. Completeness. Are all functions required by the customer included?

164. How do you know when a Requirement is accurate enough?

165. What will be the integration problems?

166. How linear / iterative is your Requirements Gathering process (or will it be)?

167. Is the requirement realistically testable?

168. Do technical resources exist?

169. What kind of entity is a problem ?

170. Is new technology needed?

2.5 Requirements Traceability Matrix: M2M IoT

171. What are the chronologies, contingencies, consequences, criteria?

172. Is there a requirements traceability process in place?

173. Why Do you Manage Scope?

174. How will it affect the stakeholders personally in their career?

175. Describe the process for approving requirements so they can be added to the traceability matrix and M2M IoT project work can be performed. Will the M2M IoT project requirements become approved in writing?

176. What is the WBS?

177. How small is small enough?

178. What percentage of M2M IoT projects are producing traceability matrices between requirements and other work products?

179. Will you use a Requirements Traceability Matrix?

180. How Do you Manage Scope?

181. Why use a WBS?

182. Do we have a clear understanding of all subcontracts in place?

2.6 Project Scope Statement: M2M IoT

183. Were key M2M IoT project stakeholders brought into the M2M IoT project Plan?

184. Have you been able to easily identify success criteria and create objective measurements for each of the M2M IoT project scopes goal statements?

185. Is there a baseline plan against which to measure progress?

186. Does the scope statement still need some clarity?

187. Will tasks be marked complete only after QA has been successfully completed?

188. Write a brief purpose statement for this M2M IoT project. Include a business justification statement. What is the product of this M2M IoT project?

189. Have the reports to be produced, distributed, and filed been defined?

190. Is the scope of your M2M IoT project well defined?

191. Will there be a Change Control Process in place?

192. Name and describe the 2 elements that deal with providing the detail?

193. How often do you estimate that the scope might change, and why?

194. Was planning completed before the M2M IoT project was initiated?

195. Have the Configuration Management functions been assigned?

196. Will the Risk Status be reported to management on a regular and frequent basis?

197. What are the defined meeting materials?

198. What is the product of this M2M IoT project?

199. How often will scope changes be reviewed?

200. Will the M2M IoT project risks being managed be according to the M2M IoT projects risk management process?

201. What is a process you might recommend to verify the accuracy of the research deliverable?

202. Is the M2M IoT project Manager qualified and experienced in M2M IoT project Management?

2.7 Assumption and Constraint Log: M2M IoT

203. When can log be discarded?

204. Security analysis has access to information that is sanitized?

205. Does the document/deliverable meet general requirements (for example, statement of work) for all deliverables?

206. Is this model reasonable?

207. Are there processes in place to ensure that all the terms and code concepts have been documented consistently?

208. Have you eliminated all duplicative tasks or manual efforts, where appropriate?

209. Contradictory information between document sections?

210. If it is out of compliance, should the process be amended or should the Plan be amended?

211. No superfluous information or marketing narrative?

212. Have all necessary approvals been obtained?

213. Does a documented M2M IoT project

organizational policy & plan (i.e. governance model) exist?

214. What to do at recovery?

215. Diagrams and tables are included to explain complex concepts and increase overall readability?

216. Does the system design reflect the requirements?

217. Should factors be unpredictable over time?

218. Violation Trace: Why ?

219. What worked well?

220. Has the approach and development strategy of the M2M IoT project been defined, documented and accepted by the appropriate stakeholders?

221. What would you gain if you spent time working to improve this process?

222. Is there adequate stakeholder participation for the vetting of requirements definition, changes and management?

2.8 Work Breakdown Structure: M2M IoT

223. What is the probability of completing the M2M IoT project in less that xx days?

224. Is it a change in scope?

225. Why would you develop a Work Breakdown Structure?

226. How many levels?

227. Who has to do it?

228. Why is it useful?

229. Is the Work breakdown Structure (WBS) defined and is the scope of the M2M IoT project clear with assigned deliverable owners?

230. When does it have to be done?

231. When would you develop a Work Breakdown Structure?

232. Is it still viable?

233. How much detail?

234. Do you need another level?

235. How Far Down?

236. When do you stop?

237. What has to be done?

238. How big is a work-package?

239. How will you and your M2M IoT project team define the M2M IoT projects scope and work breakdown structure?

240. Where does it take place?

241. What is the probability that the M2M IoT project duration will exceed xx weeks?

242. Can you make it?

2.9 WBS Dictionary: M2M IoT

243. Appropriate work authorization documents which subdivide the contractual effort and responsibilities, within functional organizations?

244. Are indirect costs accumulated for comparison with the corresponding budgets?

245. Are direct or indirect cost adjustments being accomplished according to accounting procedures acceptable to us?

246. Are overhead cost budgets (or M2M IoT projections) established on a facility-wide basis at least annually for the life of the contract?

247. Are all affected work authorizations, budgeting, and scheduling documents amended to properly reflect the effects of authorized changes?

248. What is the end result of a work package?

249. Are data elements reconcilable between internal summary reports and reports forwarded to us?

250. Does the contractors system description or procedures require that the performance measurement baseline plus management reserve equal the contract budget base?

251. Are all elements of indirect expense identified to overhead cost budgets of M2M IoT projections?

252. Is work progressively subdivided into detailed work packages as requirements are defined?

253. Are records maintained to show how management reserves are used?

254. Is the work done on a work package level as described in the WBS dictionary?

255. Are work packages assigned to performing organizations?

256. Do procedures specify under what circumstances replanning of open work packages may occur, and the methods to be followed?

257. Are overhead cost budgets established for each organization which has authority to incur overhead costs?

258. Are meaningful indicators identified for use in measuring the status of cost and schedule performance?

259. Are material costs reported within the same period as that in which BCWP is earned for that material?

260. Are the procedures for identifying indirect costs to incurring organizations, indirect cost pools, and allocating the costs from the pools to the contracts formally documented?

261. Are M2M IoT projected overhead costs in each pool and the associated direct costs used as the basis for establishing interim rates for allocating overhead

to contracts?

2.10 Schedule Management Plan: M2M IoT

262. Are target dates established for each milestone deliverable?

263. Does a documented M2M IoT project organizational policy & plan (i.e. governance model) exist?

264. Has a capability assessment been conducted?

265. Are all payments made according to the contract(s)?

266. Has a structured approach been used to break work effort into manageable components (WBS)?

267. Are the primary and secondary schedule tools defined?

268. Is there a formal process for updating the M2M IoT project baseline?

269. Are the M2M IoT project team members located locally to the users/stakeholders?

270. Were stakeholders aware and supportive of the principles and practices of modern software estimation?

271. Is the schedule updated on a periodic basis?

272. Does the M2M IoT project have a formal M2M IoT project Charter?

273. Is a process defined to measure the performance of the schedule management process itself?

274. Why Conduct Schedule Analysis?

275. How does the proposed individual meet each requirement?

276. Are M2M IoT project leaders committed to this M2M IoT project full time?

277. Can additional resources be added to subsequent tasks to reduce the durations of those tasks?

278. Have adequate resources been provided by management to ensure M2M IoT project success?

279. Who is responsible for estimating the activity durations?

2.11 Activity List: M2M IoT

280. What are the critical bottleneck activities?

281. Is there anything planned that doesn t need to be here?

282. Should you include sub-activities?

283. What did not go as well?

284. Is infrastructure setup part of your M2M IoT project?

285. What is the least expensive way to complete the M2M IoT project within 40 weeks?

286. Who will perform the work?

287. How do you determine the late start (LS) for each activity?

288. For other activities, how much delay can be tolerated?

289. What will be performed?

290. How difficult will it be to do specific activities on this M2M IoT project?

291. Where will it be performed?

292. When do the individual activities need to start and finish?

293. How can the M2M IoT project be displayed graphically to better visualize the activities?

294. What went well?

295. The WBS is developed as part of a Joint Planning session. But how do you know that youve done this right?

296. How much slack is available in the M2M IoT project?

297. What is the total time required to complete the M2M IoT project if no delays occur?

2.12 Activity Attributes: M2M IoT

298. How Do you Manage Time?

299. How Much Activity Detail Is Required?

300. Whats the general pattern here?

301. Does the organization of the data change its meaning?

302. Are the required resources available?

303. Is there a trend during the year?

304. Have you identified the Activity Leveling Priority code value on each activity?

305. Resources to accomplish the work?

306. Would you consider either of these activities an outlier?

307. Time for overtime?

308. How many days do you need to complete the work scope with a limit of X number of resources?

309. How else could the items be grouped?

310. What activity do you think you should spend the most time on?

311. Were there other ways you could have organized

the data to achieve similar results?

312. Why?

313. Activity: Fair or Not Fair?

314. What conclusions/generalizations can you draw from this?

2.13 Milestone List: M2M IoT

315. How late can the activity finish?

316. Which path is the critical path?

317. Usps (unique selling points)?

318. Identify critical paths (one or more) and which activities are on the critical path?

319. Marketing - reach, distribution, awareness?

320. Calculate how long can activity be delayed?

321. How late can each activity be finished and started?

322. Sustaining internal capabilities?

323. Who will manage the M2M IoT project on a day-to-day basis?

324. Milestone pages should display the UserID of the person who added the milestone. Does a report or query exist that provides this audit information?

325. Global influences?

326. What is the market for your technology, product or service?

327. Continuity, supply chain robustness?

328. Level of the Innovation?

329. Obstacles faced?

330. What has been done so far?

331. Reliability of data, plan predictability?

332. How will the milestone be verified?

333. Environmental effects?

334. Legislative effects?

2.14 Network Diagram: M2M IoT

335. What must be completed before an activity can be started?

336. Which type of network diagram allows you to depict four types of dependencies?

337. What activities must follow this activity?

338. Will crashing x weeks return more in benefits than it costs?

339. If X is long, what would be the completion time if you break X into two parallel parts of y weeks and z weeks?

340. If the M2M IoT project network diagram cannot change but you have extra personnel resources, what is the BEST thing to do?

341. Where Do Schedules Come From?

342. What activity must be completed immediately before this activity can start?

343. What are the tools?

344. Where do you schedule uncertainty time?

345. What is the completion time?

346. What are the Key Success Factors?

347. What job or jobs precede it?

348. If a current contract exists, can you provide the vendor name, contract start, and contract expiration date?

349. What job or jobs could run concurrently?

350. What is the probability of completing the M2M IoT project in less that xx days?

351. What is the lowest cost to complete this M2M IoT project in xx weeks?

352. Why must you schedule milestones, such as reviews, throughout the M2M IoT project?

353. Planning: who, how long, what to do?

2.15 Activity Resource Requirements: M2M IoT

354. Other support in specific areas?

355. Which logical relationship does the PDM use most often?

356. Do you use tools like decomposition and rolling-wave planning to produce the activity list and other outputs?

357. When does Monitoring Begin?

358. Why do you do that?

359. What is the Work Plan Standard?

360. How do you handle petty cash?

361. Organizational Applicability?

362. How many signatures do you require on a check and does this match what is in your policy and procedures?

363. What are constraints that you might find during the Human Resource Planning process?

364. Anything else?

365. Are there unresolved issues that need to be addressed?

2.16 Resource Breakdown Structure: M2M IoT

366. Why Do you Do It?

367. Who needs what information?

368. Any Changes from Stakeholders?

369. Which resource planning tool provides information on resource responsibility and accountability?

370. What is the organizations history in doing similar activities?

371. Which resources should be in the resource pool?

372. Who will be used as a M2M IoT project team member?

373. What is the number one predictor of a groups productivity?

374. What is the primary purpose of the human resource plan?

375. Who will use the system?

376. What can you do to improve productivity?

377. Who is allowed to perform which functions?

378. What Defines a Successful M2M IoT project?

379. When do they need the information?

380. What Is M2M IoT project Communication Management?

381. Is Predictive Resource Analysis being done?

2.17 Activity Duration Estimates: M2M IoT

382. Calculate the expected duration for an activity that has a most likely time of 5, a pessimistic time of 13, and a optimistic time of 3?

383. Does a process exist for approving or rejecting changes?

384. Are procedures defined by which the M2M IoT project scope may be changed?

385. A M2M IoT project manager is using weighted average duration estimates to perform schedule network analysis. Which type of mathematical analysis is being used?

386. What do you think the real problem was in this case?

387. Are M2M IoT project costs tracked in the general ledger?

388. Do an Internet search on earning PMP certification. Be sure to search for Yahoo Groups related to this topic. What are some of the options you found to help people prepare for the exam?

389. Does a process exist to identify M2M IoT project roles, responsibilities and reporting relationships?

390. What tasks can take place concurrently?

391. How can others help M2M IoT project managers understand the organizational context for their M2M IoT projects?

392. Which tips for taking the PMP exam do you think would be most helpful for you?

393. Are actual M2M IoT project results compared with planned or expected results to determine the variance?

394. What is the difference between conceptual, application, and evaluative questions?

395. What do such sources say about M2M IoT project management?

396. What are some of the ways to create and distribute M2M IoT project performance information?

397. Calculate the expected duration for an activity that has a most likely time of 3, a pessimistic time of 10, and a optimistic time of 2?

398. Are procedures followed to ensure information is available to stakeholders in a timely manner?

399. How have experts such as Deming, Juran, Crosby, and Taguchi affected the quality movement and todays use of Six Sigma?

400. (Cpi), and schedule performance index (spi) for the M2M IoT project?

2.18 Duration Estimating Worksheet: M2M IoT

401. What s Next?

402. What is the total time required to complete the M2M IoT project if no delays occur?

403. What is the least expensive way to complete the M2M IoT project within 40 weeks?

404. Done before proceeding with this activity or what can be done concurrently?

405. Can the M2M IoT project be constructed as planned?

406. Is the M2M IoT project responsive to community need?

407. Do any colleagues have experience with the company and/or RFPs?

408. What is your role?

409. Is a Construction detail attached (to aid in explanation)?

410. Does the M2M IoT project provide innovative ways for Veterans to overcome obstacles or deliver better outcomes?

411. When, then?

412. What utility impacts are there?

413. When does the organization expect to be able to complete it?

414. Science = Process: Remember the Scientific Method?

415. What does it mean to say a task is 75% complete after 3 months?

416. What info is needed?

417. What questions do you have?

2.19 Project Schedule: M2M IoT

418. Are key risk mitigation strategies added to the M2M IoT project schedule?

419. If you can t fix it, how do you do it differently?

420. Should you have a test for each code module?

421. Did the final product meet or exceed user expectations?

422. What are you counting on?

423. To what degree is do you feel the entire team was committed to the M2M IoT project schedule?

424. Verify that the update is accurate. Are all remaining durations correct?

425. How can you fix it?

426. Are quality inspections and review activities listed in the M2M IoT project schedule(s)?

427. How effectively were issues able to be resolved without impacting the M2M IoT project Schedule or Budget?

428. What is the most mis-scheduled part of process?

429. How Do you Use Schedules?

430. How do you manage M2M IoT project Risk?

431. Meet requirements?

432. How can you shorten the schedule?

433. Is the structure for tracking the M2M IoT project schedule well defined and assigned to a specific individual?

434. Eliminate unnecessary activities. Are there activities that came from a template or previous M2M IoT project that are not applicable on this phase of this M2M IoT project?

435. Activity charts and bar charts are graphical representations of a M2M IoT project schedule ...how do they differ?

436. What is Risk?

437. How detailed should a M2M IoT project get?

2.20 Cost Management Plan: M2M IoT

438. Is the M2M IoT project schedule available for all M2M IoT project team members to review?

439. Are any non-compliance issues that exist due to State practices communicated to the State?

440. What would you do differently what did not work?

441. Are the schedule estimates reasonable given the M2M IoT project?

442. Scope of work – What is the likelihood and extent of potential future changes to the M2M IoT project scope?

443. If you sold 11 widgets on day, what would the affect on profits be?

444. Cost / Benefit Analysis?

445. Does the schedule include M2M IoT project management time and change request analysis time?

446. Are cause and effect determined for risks when others occur?

447. Is there an approved case?

448. M2M IoT project Definition & Scope?

449. Contingency rundown curve be used on the

M2M IoT project?

450. Is M2M IoT project work proceeding in accordance with the original M2M IoT project schedule?

451. How difficult will it be to do specific tasks on the M2M IoT project?

452. Do M2M IoT project teams & team members report on status / activities / progress?

453. Are decisions captured in a decisions log?

454. Were the budget estimates reasonable?

455. Has a M2M IoT project Communications Plan been developed?

2.21 Activity Cost Estimates: M2M IoT

456. What cost data should be used to estimate costs during the 2-year follow-up period?

457. How and when do you enter into M2M IoT project Procurement Management?

458. Maintenance Reserve?

459. Were decisions made in a timely manner?

460. Was the consultant knowledgeable about the program?

461. Will you use any tools, such as M2M IoT project management software, to assist in capturing Earned Value metrics?

462. Specific - Is the objective clear in terms of what, how, when, and where the situation will be changed?

463. What Defines a Successful M2M IoT project?

464. How do you treat administrative costs in the activity inventory?

465. What is the activity inventory?

466. Eac -estimate at completion, what is the total job expected to cost?

467. What is the last item a M2M IoT project manager must do to finalize M2M IoT project close-out?

468. How quickly can the task be done with the skills available?

469. Will you need to provide essential services information about activities?

470. What procedures are put in place regarding bidding and cost comparisons, if any?

471. Were sponsors and decision makers available when needed outside regularly scheduled meetings?

472. What are the audit requirements?

473. What is a M2M IoT project Management Plan?

474. What is the estimators estimating history?

2.22 Cost Estimating Worksheet: M2M IoT

475. What additional M2M IoT project(s) could be initiated as a result of this M2M IoT project?

476. How will the results be shared and to whom?

477. What costs are to be estimated?

478. Is the M2M IoT project responsive to community need?

479. Value Pocket Identification & Quantification What Are Value Pockets?

480. What Can Be Included?

481. Can a trend be established from historical performance data on the selected measure and are the criteria for using trend analysis or forecasting methods met?

482. Ask: are others positioned to know, are others credible, and will others cooperate?

483. What happens to any remaining funds not used?

484. What is the purpose of estimating?

485. Is it feasible to establish a control group arrangement?

486. What will others want?

487. Will the M2M IoT project collaborate with the local community and leverage resources?

488. What is the estimated labor cost today based upon this information?

489. Who is best positioned to know and assist in identifying such factors?

490. Identify the timeframe necessary to monitor progress and collect data to determine how the selected measure has changed?

491. Does the M2M IoT project provide innovative ways for stakeholders to overcome obstacles or deliver better outcomes?

2.23 Cost Baseline: M2M IoT

492. Does it impact schedule, cost, quality?

493. Have the resources used by the M2M IoT project been reassigned to other units or M2M IoT projects?

494. What Strengths do you have?

495. Vac -variance at completion, how much over/ under budget do you expect to be?

496. Will the M2M IoT project fail if the change request is not executed?

497. When should cost estimates be developed?

498. On budget?

499. What s the reality?

500. At which frequency ?

501. Has operations management formally accepted responsibility for operating and maintaining the product(s) or service(s) delivered by the M2M IoT project?

502. What is the organization s history in doing similar tasks?

503. How long are you willing to wait before you find out were late?

504. Has training and knowledge transfer of the operations organization been completed?

505. How will cost estimates be used?

506. Escalation Criteria Met?

507. What Threats might prevent us from getting there?

508. Does the suggested change request represent a desired enhancement to the products functionality?

2.24 Quality Management Plan: M2M IoT

509. How does your organization address regulatory, legal, and ethical compliance?

510. What are your organizations current levels and trends for those measures related to employee wellbeing, satisfaction, and development?

511. What has the QM Collaboration done?

512. What data do you gather/use/compile?

513. Are you following the quality standards?

514. What is the Quality Management Plan?

515. What is positive about the current process?

516. Diagrams and tables to explain complex concepts and increase overall readability?

517. How do your action plans support the strategic objectives?

518. What are your organizations key processes (product, service, business, and support)?

519. What is the return on investment?

520. How do you check in-coming sample material?

521. How do senior leaders create an environment that encourages learning and innovation?

522. What are the appropriate test methods to be used?

523. Were there any deficiencies / issues identified in the prior years self-assessment?

524. How are changes recorded?

525. Do the data quality objectives communicate the intended program need?

526. How do you decide what information to record?

527. How will you know that a change is actually an improvement?

528. Who is responsible?

2.25 Quality Metrics: M2M IoT

529. Filter Visualizations of Interest?

530. Product Availability ?

531. Should a modifier be included?

532. Were number of defects identified?

533. Are there any open risk issues?

534. Were quality attributes reported?

535. Which report did you use to create the data you are submitting?

536. Are documents on hand to provide explanations of privacy and confidentiality?

537. When is the security analysis testing complete?

538. Do the operators focus on determining; is there anything I need to worry about?

539. Is a risk containment plan in place?

540. How effective are your security tests?

541. Are quality metrics defined?

542. Where is Quality Now?

543. What can manufacturing professionals do to

ensure quality is seen as an integral part of the entire product lifecycle?

544. Did the team meet the M2M IoT project success criteria documented in the Quality Metrics Matrix?

545. Was review conducted per standard protocols?

546. What do you measure?

547. Is the reporting frequency appropriate?

548. What forces exist that would cause them to change?

2.26 Process Improvement Plan: M2M IoT

549. The motive is determined by asking, Why do I want to achieve this goal?

550. Why do you want to achieve the goal?

551. To elicit goal statements, do you ask a question such as, What do you want to achieve?

552. What personnel are the champions for the initiative?

553. Where are you now?

554. What personnel are the sponsors for that initiative?

555. If a Process Improvement Framework Is Being Used, Which Elements Will Help the Problems and Goals Listed?

556. How do you measure?

557. Have the supporting tools been developed or acquired?

558. What makes people good SPI coaches?

559. Everyone agrees on what process improvement is, right?

560. Have the frequency of collection and the points in the process where measurements will be made been determined?

561. What Is the Test-Cycle Concept?

562. Purpose of Goal: The motive is determined by asking, Why do I want to achieve this goal?

563. Are you meeting the quality standards?

564. What personnel are the change agents for your initiative?

565. Are you Making Progress on the Goals?

566. Where do you focus?

567. Does our process ensure quality?

2.27 Responsibility Assignment Matrix: M2M IoT

568. The anticipated business volume?

569. Does each activity-deliverable have exactly one Accountable responsibility, so that accountability is clear and decisions can be made quickly?

570. Performance to date and material commitment?

571. Are the bases and rates for allocating costs from each indirect pool consistently applied?

572. Those responsible for the establishment of budgets and assignment of resources for overhead performance?

573. Do all the identified groups or people really need to be consulted?

574. How many hours by each staff member/rate?

575. Why cost benefit analysis?

576. Do work packages consist of discrete tasks which are adequately described?

577. Budgeted cost for work scheduled?

578. The staff interests – is the group or the person interested in working for this M2M IoT project?

579. Which M2M IoT project Management Knowledge Area is Least Mature?

580. What travel needed?

581. Does each role with Accountable responsibility have the authority within the organization to make the required decisions?

582. Authorization to proceed with all authorized work?

583. All CWBS elements specified for external reporting?

584. Is the entire contract planned in time-phased control accounts to the extent practicable?

2.28 Roles and Responsibilities: M2M IoT

585. What expectations were NOT met?

586. Once the responsibilities are defined for the M2M IoT project, have the deliverables, roles and responsibilities been clearly communicated to every participant?

587. Are M2M IoT project team roles and responsibilities identified and documented?

588. Key conclusions and recommendations: Are conclusions and recommendations relevant and acceptable?

589. Are our policies supportive of a culture of quality data?

590. Attainable / Achievable: The goal is attainable; can you actually accomplish the goal?

591. What should you do now to prepare for your career 5+ years from now?

592. What expectations were met?

593. Whats working well?

594. Is feedback clearly communicated and non-judgmental?

595. Accountabilities: What are the roles and responsibilities of individual team members?

596. What areas would you highlight for changes or improvements?

597. Who is responsible for implementation activities and where will the functions, roles and responsibilities be defined?

598. What areas of supervision are challenging for you?

599. Concern: where are you limited or have no authority, where you cant influence?

600. What specific behaviors did you observe?

601. Does our vision/mission support a culture of quality data?

602. To decide whether to use a quality measurement, ask how will I know when it is achieved?

603. Are governance roles and responsibilities documented?

604. Does the team have access to and ability to use data analysis tools?

2.29 Human Resource Management Plan: M2M IoT

605. What commitments have been made?

606. Are corrective actions and variances reported?

607. Has a provision been made to reassess M2M IoT project risks at various M2M IoT project stages?

608. Are software metrics formally captured, analyzed and used as a basis for other M2M IoT project estimates?

609. List the assumptions made to date. What did you have to assume to be true to complete the charter?

610. Does the schedule include M2M IoT project management time and change request analysis time?

611. Are meeting minutes captured and sent out after the meeting?

612. Are tasks tracked by hours?

613. Is a PMO (M2M IoT project Management Office) in place and provide oversight to the M2M IoT project?

614. Sensitivity analysis?

615. Is the company heading towards expansion, outsourcing of certain talents or making cut-backs to save money?

616. Timeline and milestones?

617. Does the M2M IoT project have a Statement of Work?

618. Quality Assurance overheads?

619. Are staff skills known and available for each task?

620. Have stakeholder accountabilities & responsibilities been clearly defined?

621. Is there general agreement & acceptance of the current status and progress of the M2M IoT project?

2.30 Communications Management Plan: M2M IoT

622. What approaches do you use?

623. Are you constantly rushing from meeting to meeting?

624. Are others needed?

625. Who were proponents/opponents?

626. Who have you worked with in past, similar initiatives?

627. Are the stakeholders getting the information others need, are others consulted, are concerns addressed?

628. How much time does it take to do it?

629. Are stakeholders internal or external?

630. Why Do you Manage Communications?

631. Conflict Resolution -which method when?

632. What to learn?

633. Do you then often overlook a key stakeholder or stakeholder group?

634. Who will use or be affected by the result of a

M2M IoT project?

635. Is the stakeholder role recognized by the organization?

636. Will messages be directly related to the release strategy or phases of the M2M IoT project?

637. Who needs to know and how much?

638. Is there an important stakeholder who is actively opposed and will not receive messages?

639. Why Manage Stakeholders?

640. Do you feel a register helps?

2.31 Risk Management Plan: M2M IoT

641. Could others have been better mitigated?

642. If you cant fix it, how do you do it differently?

643. Is there additional information that would make you more confident about your analysis?

644. Is the customer willing to participate in reviews?

645. What can go wrong?

646. Has something like this been done before?

647. What are the chances the risk event will occur?

648. Are M2M IoT project requirements stable?

649. Are tool mentors available?

650. Is the customer willing to commit significant time to the requirements gathering process?

651. Does the M2M IoT project team have experience with the technology to be implemented?

652. Market risk -Will the new service or product be useful to the organization or marketable to others?

653. My M2M IoT project leader has suddenly left the company, what do I do?

654. Do the people have the right combinations of

skills?

655. Was an original risk assessment/risk management plan completed?

656. What are the chances the event will occur?

657. How do you manage M2M IoT project Risk?

658. Anticipated volatility of the requirements?

659. Why Is Product Liability a Serious Issue?

660. Who has experience with this?

2.32 Risk Register: M2M IoT

661. Who is accountable?

662. Assume the event happens, what is the Most Likely impact?

663. When is it going to be done?

664. How are Risks Identified?

665. What may happen or not go according to plan?

666. Which key risks have ineffective responses or outstanding improvement actions?

667. What are you going to do to limit the M2M IoT projects risk exposure due to the identified risks?

668. What is a Community Risk Register?

669. Amongst the action plans and recommendations that you have to introduce are there some that could stop or delay the overall program?

670. What would the impact to the M2M IoT project objectives be should the risk arise?

671. Having taken action, how did the responses effect change, and where is the M2M IoT project now?

672. When would you develop a risk register?

673. What could prevent us delivering on the strategic

program objectives and what is being done to mitigate such issues?

674. Technology risk -is the M2M IoT project technically feasible?

675. What should you do now?

676. What Should The Audit Role Be In Establishing a Risk Management Process?

677. Whats the appropriate level of risk management for this M2M IoT project?

678. Are there any gaps in the evidence?

679. What are the assumptions and current status that support the assessment of the risk?

2.33 Probability and Impact Assessment: M2M IoT

680. Your customer's business requirements have suddenly shifted because of a new regulatory statute, what now?

681. Supply/demand M2M IoT projections and trends; what are the levels of accuracy?

682. Are there any M2M IoT projects similar to this one in existence?

683. How much risk do others need to take?

684. What are the tools and techniques used in managing the challenges faced?

685. What are the preparations required for facing difficulties?

686. What are the levels of understanding of the future users of the outcome/results of this M2M IoT project?

687. Is the process supported by tools?

688. Are the best people available?

689. Can this technology be absorbed with current level of expertise available in the organization?

690. What is the impact if the risk does occur?

691. Does the customer have a solid idea of what is required?

692. To what extent is the chosen technology maturing?

693. Are flexibility and reuse paramount?

694. What will be cost of redeployment of personnel?

695. What is the past performance of the M2M IoT project manager?

696. How solid is the M2M IoT projection of competitive reaction?

697. Do you use diagramming techniques to show cause and effect?

698. Do requirements put excessive performance constraints on the product?

2.34 Probability and Impact Matrix: M2M IoT

699. How should you structure risks?

700. How carefully have the potential competitors been identified?

701. What will be the environmental impact of the M2M IoT project?

702. Do you use any methods to analyze risks?

703. How well is the risk understood?

704. What kind of preparation would be required to do this?

705. What will be cost of redeployment of the personnel?

706. Is the present organizational structure for handling the M2M IoT project sufficient?

707. What are the uncertainties associated with the technology selected for the M2M IoT project?

708. Premium on reliability of product?

709. Are M2M IoT project requirements stable?

710. What will be the likely incidence of conflict with neighboring M2M IoT projects?

711. Mandated delivery date?

712. What are its business ethics?

713. Does the software engineering team have the right mix of skills?

714. What are the current requirements of the customer?

715. Workarounds are determined during which step of risk management?

2.35 Risk Data Sheet: M2M IoT

716. Risk of What?

717. How can it happen?

718. What actions can be taken to eliminate or remove risk?

719. Potential for Recurrence?

720. Is the data sufficiently specified in terms of the type of failure being analysed, and its frequency or probability?

721. Are new hazards created?

722. During work activities could hazards exist?

723. What were the Causes that contributed?

724. Who has a vested interest in how you perform as an organization (our stakeholders)?

725. Has a sensitivity analysis been carried out?

726. What can YOU do?

727. Do effective diagnostic tests exist?

728. Has the most cost-effective solution been chosen?

729. How do you handle product safely?

730. Whom do you serve (customers)?

731. What can happen?

732. What is the environment within which you operate (social trends, economic, community values, broad based participation, national directions etc.)?

733. What was Measured?

734. If it happens, what are the consequences?

735. What do people affected think about the need for, and practicality of preventive measures?

2.36 Procurement Management Plan: M2M IoT

736. Have all involved M2M IoT project stakeholders and work groups committed to the M2M IoT project?

737. What types of contracts will be used?

738. Based on your M2M IoT project communication management plan, what worked well?

739. M2M IoT project Objectives?

740. Has the M2M IoT project manager been identified?

741. Do all stakeholders know how to access the PM repository and where to find the M2M IoT project documentation?

742. Are procurement deliverables arriving on time and to specification?

743. Does the schedule include M2M IoT project management time and change request analysis time?

744. Financial capacity; does the seller have, or can the seller reasonably be expected to obtain, the financial resources needed?

745. Were M2M IoT project team members involved in the development of activity & task decomposition?

746. Are meeting objectives identified for each meeting?

747. Alignment to strategic goals & objectives?

748. Are milestone deliverables effectively tracked and compared to M2M IoT project plan?

749. How and when do you enter into M2M IoT project Procurement Management?

750. Are individual tasks of reasonable time effort (8–40 hours)?

751. Are Vendor contract reports, reviews and visits conducted periodically?

752. Are the budget estimates reasonable?

2.37 Source Selection Criteria: M2M IoT

753. How should the preproposal conference be conducted?

754. What documentation is needed for a tradeoff decision?

755. Does the evaluation of any change include an impact analysis; how will the change affect the scope, time, cost, and quality of the goods or services being provided?

756. Can you reasonably estimate total organization requirements for the coming year?

757. What are the guidelines regarding award without discussions?

758. Is the contracting office likely to receive more purchase requests for this item or service during the coming year?

759. Are there any specific considerations that precludes offers from being selected as the awardee?

760. Are there any common areas of weaknesses or deficiencies in the proposals in the competitive range?

761. What instructions should be provided regarding oral presentations?

762. Comparison of each offer's prices to the estimated prices -are there significant differences?

763. What should clarifications include?

764. What should a Draft Request for Proposal (DRFP) include?

765. What Should Be Discussed?

766. What documentation should be used to support the selection decision?

767. What procedures are followed when a contractor requires access to classified information or a significant quantity of special material/information?

768. How are oral presentations documented?

769. What are the most critical evaluation criteria that prove to be tiebreakers in the evaluation of proposals?

770. How much past performance information should be requested?

771. How can business terms and conditions be improved to yield more effective price competition?

772. Are Resultant Proposal Revisions Allowed?

2.38 Stakeholder Management Plan: M2M IoT

773. Who is responsible for the post implementation review process?

774. How is information analyzed, and what specific pieces of data would be of interest to the M2M IoT project manager?

775. Are the M2M IoT project team members located locally to the users/stakeholders?

776. Who will be collecting information?

777. Is there a formal process for updating the M2M IoT project baseline?

778. Has a M2M IoT project Communications Plan been developed?

779. Are communication systems proposed compatible with staff skills and experience?

780. Have the key elements of a coherent M2M IoT project management strategy been established?

781. Are actuals compared against estimates to analyze and correct variances?

782. Are changes in scope (deliverable commitments) agreed to by all affected groups & individuals?

783. At what point will the M2M IoT project be closed and what will be done to formally close the M2M IoT project?

784. Are risk oriented checklists used during risk identification?

785. Is it standard practice to formally commit stakeholders to the M2M IoT project via agreements?

786. What proven methodologies and standards will be used to ensure that materials, products, processes and services are fit for their purpose?

787. Are M2M IoT project leaders committed to this M2M IoT project full time?

788. What is meant by activity dependencies and how do they relate to network diagramming?

789. After observing execution of process, is it in compliance with the documented Plan?

790. Are communication systems currently in place appropriate?

791. Does the M2M IoT project have a formal M2M IoT project Charter?

2.39 Change Management Plan: M2M IoT

792. Has an Information & communications plan been developed?

793. Is there an adequate supply of people for the new roles?

794. What are the training strategies?

795. Will a different work structure focus people on what is important?

796. Have the approved procedures and policies been published?

797. Is there a support model for this application and are the details available for distribution?

798. How prevalent is Resistance to Change?

799. What do you expect the target audience to do, say, think or feel as a result of this communication?

800. What are the essentials of the message?

801. What type of materials/channels will be available to leverage?

802. Do the proposed users have access to the appropriate documentation?

803. Who might present the most resistance?

804. What communication network would you use – informal or formal?

805. How can you best frame the message so that it addresses the audiences interests?

806. Who might be able to help us the most?

807. Where do you want to be?

808. How does the principle of senders and receivers make the M2M IoT project communications effort more complex?

809. Has the Training co-ordinator been provided with the training details and put in place the necessary arrangements?

810. Change invariability confront many relationships especially those that require a set of behaviours What roles with in the organization are affected and how?

3.0 Executing Process Group: M2M IoT

811. How could stakeholders negatively impact your M2M IoT project?

812. Is the programme supported by national and/or local institutions?

813. How does a M2M IoT project life cycle differ from a product life cycle?

814. How can software assist in M2M IoT project communications?

815. Who will provide training?

816. Is activity definition the first process involved in M2M IoT project time management?

817. What are the challenges M2M IoT project teams face?

818. Why is it important to determine activity sequencing on M2M IoT projects?

819. Do the products created live up to the necessary quality?

820. Will a new application be developed using existing hardware, software, and networks?

821. How will professionals learn what is expected from them what the deliverables are?

822. What were things that you need to improve?

823. What are the key components of the M2M IoT project communications plan?

824. What were things that you did very well and want to do the same again on the next M2M IoT project?

825. Does the case present a realistic scenario?

826. How could you control progress of your M2M IoT project?

3.1 Team Member Status Report: M2M IoT

827. Are the attitudes of staff regarding M2M IoT project work improving?

828. Will the staff do training or is that done by a third party?

829. How it is to be done?

830. What specific interest groups do you have in place?

831. What is to be done?

832. Do you have an Enterprise M2M IoT project Management Office (EPMO)?

833. The problem with Reward & Recognition Programs is that the truly deserving people all too often get left out. How can you make it practical?

834. Are the organization's M2M IoT projects more successful over time?

835. When a teams productivity and success depend on collaboration and the efficient flow of information, what generally fails them?

836. Does the organization have the means (staff, money, contract, etc.) to produce or to acquire the product, good, or service?

837. Why is it to be done?

838. How does this product, good, or service meet the needs of the M2M IoT project and the organization as a whole?

839. Are the products of the organization's M2M IoT projects meeting their customer's objectives?

840. How will Resource Planning be done?

841. How much risk is involved?

842. How can you make it practical?

843. Does the product, good, or service already exist within the organization?

844. Does every department have to have a M2M IoT project Manager on staff?

845. Is there evidence that staff is taking a more professional approach toward management of the organizations M2M IoT projects?

3.2 Change Request: M2M IoT

846. Have SCM procedures for noting the change, recording it, and reporting it been followed?

847. Are you Implementing ITIL Processes?

848. How are the measures for carrying out the change established?

849. Since there are no change requests in your M2M IoT project at this point, what must you have before you begin?

850. What has an inspector to inspect and to check?

851. Screen shots or attachments included in a Change Request?

852. Will all change requests be unconditionally tracked through this process?

853. How are changes requested (forms, method of communication)?

854. What is the change request log?

855. Which requirements attributes affect the risk to reliability the most?

856. Who needs to approve change requests?

857. What is the function of the change control committee?

858. Will all change requests and current status be logged?

859. What are the Impacts to an organization?

860. How can changes be graded?

861. Are there requirements attributes that are strongly related to the complexity and size?

862. Who Will Perform the Change?

863. How can you ensure that changes have been made properly?

864. Describe how modifications, enhancements, defects and/or deficiencies shall be notified (e.g. Problem Reports, Change Requests etc) and managed. Detail warranty and/or maintenance periods?

865. Should a more thorough impact analysis be conducted?

3.3 Change Log: M2M IoT

866. Is the submitted change a new change or a modification of a previously approved change?

867. Is this a mandatory replacement?

868. Is the requested change request a result of changes in other M2M IoT project(s)?

869. Who initiated the change request?

870. Is the change backward compatible without limitations?

871. Will the M2M IoT project fail if the change request is not executed?

872. How does this change affect scope?

873. How does this relate to the standards developed for specific business processes?

874. Do the described changes impact on the integrity or security of the system?

875. How does this change affect the timeline of the schedule?

876. Where Do Changes Come From?

877. When was the request submitted?

878. Does the suggested change request seem to

represent a necessary enhancement to the product?

879. Is the change request open, closed or pending?

880. Is the change request within M2M IoT project scope?

881. When was the request approved?

3.4 Decision Log: M2M IoT

882. What is your overall strategy for quality control / quality assurance procedures?

883. With whom was the decision shared or discussed?

884. Meeting purpose; why does this team meet?

885. What is the average size of your matters in an applicable measurement?

886. Which variables make a critical difference?

887. Does anything need to be adjusted?

888. How does the use a Decision Support System influence the strategies/tactics or costs?

889. Is everything working as expected?

890. What makes you different or better than others companies selling the same thing?

891. It becomes critical to track and periodically revisit both operational effectiveness; Are you noticing all that you need to, and are you interpreting what you see effectively?

892. How consolidated and comprehensive a story can we tell by capturing currently available incident data in a central location and through a log of key decisions during an incident?

893. At what point in time does loss become unacceptable?

894. What was the rationale for the decision?

895. How effective is maintaining the log at facilitating organizational learning?

896. Who will be given a copy of this document and where will it be kept?

897. How does an increasing emphasis on cost containment influence the strategies and tactics used?

898. How does provision of information, both in terms of content and presentation, influence acceptance of alternative strategies?

899. Linked to original objective?

900. Decision-making process; how will the team make decisions?

901. Who is the decisionmaker?

3.5 Quality Audit: M2M IoT

902. How do staff know if they are doing a good job?

903. How does the organization know that its staff entrance standards are appropriately effective and constructive and being implemented consistently?

904. How does the organization know that its policy management system is appropriately effective and constructive?

905. How does the organization know that its system for recruiting the best staff possible are appropriately effective and constructive?

906. How does the organization know that its general support services planning and management systems are appropriately effective and constructive?

907. How does the organization know that it provides a safe and healthy environment?

908. Does the suppliers quality system have a written procedure for corrective action when a defect occurs?

909. Will the evidence likely be sufficient and appropriate?

910. Is the continuing professional education of key personnel explained in detail?

911. How does the organization know that its quality of teaching is appropriately effective and

constructive?

912. Are storage areas and reconditioning operations designed to prevent mix-ups and assure orderly handling of both the distressed and reconditioned devices?

913. How does the organization know that its relationships with the community at large are appropriately effective and constructive?

914. How does your organization know that the review processes are effective?

915. How does the organization know that its staff support services planning and management systems are appropriately effective and constructive?

916. Is the process of self review, learning and improvement endemic throughout the organization?

917. How does the organization know that its system for inducting new staff to maximize their workplace contributions are appropriately effective and constructive?

918. How does the organization know that the research supervision provided to its staff is appropriately effective and constructive?

919. Are all records associated with the reconditioning of a device maintained for a minimum of two years after the sale or disposal of the last device within a lot of merchandise?

920. How does the organization know that its

methods are appropriately effective and constructive?

921. How does the organization know that its system for governing staff behaviour is appropriately effective and constructive?

3.6 Team Directory: M2M IoT

922. Who will write the meeting minutes and distribute?

923. Process Decisions: Do invoice amounts match accepted work in place?

924. Timing: when do the effects of communication take place?

925. How do unidentified risks impact the outcome of the M2M IoT project?

926. How does the team resolve conflicts and ensure tasks are completed?

927. When does information need to be distributed?

928. Process Decisions: Is work progressing on schedule and per contract requirements?

929. Have you decided when to celebrate the M2M IoT projects completion date?

930. How will the team handle changes?

931. Who will talk to the customer?

932. Contract requirements complied with?

933. What needs to be communicated?

934. Who will report M2M IoT project status to all

stakeholders?

935. Decisions: What could be done better to improve the quality of the constructed product?

936. Where will the product be used and/or delivered or built when appropriate?

937. Who are your stakeholders (customers, sponsors, end users, team members)?

938. Who are the Team Members?

939. Process Decisions: Are all issues being addressed to the satisfaction of both parties within approximately 30 days from the time the issue is identified?

940. When will you produce deliverables?

941. Who should receive information (all stakeholders)?

3.7 Team Operating Agreement: M2M IoT

942. Reimbursements: How will the team members be reimbursed for expenses and time commitments?

943. Did you prepare participants for the next meeting?

944. Confidentiality: How will confidential information be handled?

945. Have you established procedures that team members can follow to work effectively together, such as a team operating agreement?

946. Methodologies: How will key team processes be implemented, such as training, research, work deliverable production, review and approval processes, knowledge management, and meeting procedures?

947. The method to be used in the decision making process; Will it be consensus, majority rule, or the supervisor having the final say?

948. Did you recap the meeting purpose, time, and expectations?

949. Did you determine the technology methods that best match the messages to be communicated?

950. What is Culture?

951. Do you ask participants to close their laptops and place their mobile devices on silent on the table while the meeting is in progress?

952. What is Group Supervision?

953. What are the safety issues/risks that need to be addressed and/or that the team needs to discuss?

954. Do you begin with a question to engage everyone?

955. Do you post any action items, due dates, and responsibilities on the team website?

956. What is a Virtual Team?

957. How will your group handle planned absences?

958. Do you leverage technology engagement tools group chat, polls, screen sharing, etc.?

959. Do you call or email participants to ensure understanding, follow-through and commitment to the meeting outcomes?

960. How will you resolve conflict efficiently and respectfully?

961. Do you ask one question at a time and wait 10 seconds for members to respond?

3.8 Team Performance Assessment: M2M IoT

962. What structural changes have you made or are you preparing to make?

963. To what degree does the team possess adequate membership to achieve its ends?

964. To what degree do the goals specify concrete team work products?

965. To what degree are the goals ambitious?

966. To what degree do team members understand one anothers roles and skills?

967. To what degree can team members vigorously define the teams purpose in discussions with others who are not part of the functioning team?

968. To what degree are the relative importance and priority of the goals clear to all team members?

969. If you have criticized someones work for method variance in your role as reviewer, what was the circumstance?

970. To what degree are the members clear on what they are individually responsible for and what they are jointly responsible for?

971. What are you doing specifically to develop the

leaders around you?

972. Delaying Market Entry: How Long Is too Long?

973. Where to from here?

974. To what degree does the teams work approach provide opportunity for members to engage in open interaction?

975. To what degree are staff involved as partners in the improvement process?

976. To what degree do team members frequently explore the teams purpose and its implications?

977. Can familiarity breed backup?

978. Social categorization and intergroup behaviour: Does minimal intergroup discrimination make social identity more positive?

979. What is method variance?

980. Does more radicalness mean more perceived benefits?

981. To what degree can team members frequently and easily communicate with one another?

3.9 Team Member Performance Assessment: M2M IoT

982. What instructional strategies were developed/ incorporated (e.g., direct instruction, indirect instruction, experiential learning, independent study, interactive instruction)?

983. How does your team work together?

984. To what degree can team members meet frequently enough to accomplish the teams ends?

985. What are Best Practices in use for the Performance Measurement System?

986. Where can team members go for more detailed information on performance measurement and assessment?

987. To what degree are the goals realistic?

988. What, if any, steps are available for employees who feel they have been unfairly or inaccurately rated?

989. Are assessment validation activities performed?

990. What entity leads the process, selects a potential restructuring option and develops the plan?

991. What resources do you need?

992. What evaluation results do you have?

993. To what degree are the teams goals and objectives clear, simple, and measurable?

994. Should a Ratee get a copy of all the Raters documents about the employees performance?

995. What are the basic principles and objectives of performance measurement and assessment?

996. Who they are?

997. What types of learning are targeted (e.g., cognitive, affective, psychomotor, procedural)?

998. Goals met?

999. What is a general description of the processes under performance measurement and assessment?

1000. To what degree do team members articulate the teams work approach?

1001. To what degree does the teams purpose contain themes that are particularly meaningful and memorable?

3.10 Issue Log: M2M IoT

1002. What does the stakeholder need from the team?

1003. Do you prepare stakeholder engagement plans?

1004. Do you feel more overwhelmed by stakeholders?

1005. What help do you and your team need from the stakeholders?

1006. Where do team members get their information?

1007. Can an impact cause deviation beyond team, stage or M2M IoT project tolerances?

1008. Are there too many who have an interest in some aspect of your work?

1009. Why Do you Manage Human Resources?

1010. Which stakeholders can influence others?

1011. What steps can you take for positive relationships?

1012. What are the typical contents?

1013. Are the stakeholders getting the information they need, are they consulted, are their concerns addressed?

1014. Are there potential barriers between the team

and the stakeholder?

1015. Why not more evaluators?

1016. Persistence; will users learn a work around or will they be bothered every time?

1017. How Do you Manage Human Resources?

1018. In classifying stakeholders, which approach to do so are you using?

4.0 Monitoring and Controlling Process Group: M2M IoT

1019. What good practices or successful experiences or transferable examples have been identified?

1020. User: Who wants the information and what are they interested in?

1021. But Did It Work?

1022. Purpose: Toward what end is the evaluation being conducted?

1023. Did you implement the program as designed?

1024. Overall, how does the program function to serve the clients?

1025. How were collaborations developed, and how are they sustained?

1026. How well did the chosen processes fit the needs of the M2M IoT project?

1027. What is the timeline?

1028. Is it what was agreed upon?

1029. Based on your M2M IoT project communication management plan, what worked well?

1030. What kinds of things in particular are you

looking for data on?

1031. If a risk event occurs, what will you do?

1032. Does the solution fit in with organizations technical architectural requirements?

1033. Mitigate. What will you do to minimize the impact should a risk event occur?

1034. What departments are involved in its daily operation?

1035. How should their needs be met?

4.1 Project Performance Report: M2M IoT

1036. To what degree do individual skills and abilities match task demands?

1037. To what degree can team members meet frequently enough to accomplish the team's ends?

1038. To what degree will new and supplemental skills be introduced as the need is recognized?

1039. To what degree does the team's work approach provide opportunity for members to engage in fact-based problem solving?

1040. To what degree are the demands of the task compatible with and converge with the relationships of the informal organization?

1041. To what degree does the funding match the requirement?

1042. To what degree do members articulate the goals beyond the team membership?

1043. To what degree do the relationships of the informal organization motivate task- relevant behavior and facilitate task completion?

1044. To what degree does the team's approach to its work allow for modification and improvement over time?

1045. To what degree does the information network communicate information relevant to the task?

1046. To what degree does the team's purpose contain themes that are particularly meaningful and memorable?

1047. To what degree can team members vigorously define the team's purpose in discussions with others who are not part of the functioning team?

1048. To what degree does the information network provide individuals with the information they require?

1049. To what degree can the team measure progress against specific goals?

1050. To what degree will each member have the opportunity to advance his or her professional skills in all three of the above categories while contributing to the accomplishment of the team's purpose and goals?

1051. To what degree does the task meet individual needs?

1052. To what degree are sub-teams possible or necessary?

1053. To what degree is the team cognizant of small wins to be celebrated along the way?

4.2 Variance Analysis: M2M IoT

1054. Why do variances exist?

1055. Who is generally responsible for monitoring and taking action on variances?

1056. Does the scheduling system identify in a timely manner the status of work?

1057. Are there quarterly budgets with quarterly performance comparisons?

1058. What are the actual costs to date?

1059. What can be the cause of an increase in costs?

1060. What is the expected future profitability of each customer?

1061. How does the use of a single conversion element (rather than the traditional labor and overhead elements) affect standard costing?

1062. Are the requirements for all items of overhead established by rational, traceable processes?

1063. Are procedures for variance analysis documented and consistently applied at the control account level and selected WBS and organizational levels at least monthly as a routine task?

1064. Are detailed work packages planned as far in advance as practicable?

1065. How are variances affected by multiple material and labor categories?

1066. Is the anticipated (firm and potential) business base M2M IoT projected in a rational, consistent manner?

1067. What should management do?

1068. Does the contractors system include procedures for measuring the performance of critical subcontractors?

1069. Are estimates of costs at completion generated in a rational, consistent manner?

1070. How do you identify potential or actual overruns and underruns?

1071. Contemplated overhead expenditure for each period based on the best information currently is available?

1072. Do the rates and prices remain constant throughout the year?

4.3 Earned Value Status: M2M IoT

1073. Validation is a process of ensuring that the developed system will actually achieve the stakeholders desired outcomes; Are you building the right product? What do you validate?

1074. How much is it going to cost by the finish?

1075. Where is Evidence-based Earned Value in your organization reported?

1076. When is it going to finish?

1077. Are you hitting your M2M IoT projects targets?

1078. Earned Value can be used in almost any M2M IoT project situation and in almost any M2M IoT project environment. It may be used on large M2M IoT projects, medium sized M2M IoT projects, tiny M2M IoT projects (in cut-down form), complex and simple M2M IoT projects and in any market sector. Some people, of course, know all about earned value, they have used it for years - but perhaps not as effectively as they could have?

1079. If earned value management (EVM) is so good in determining the true status of a M2M IoT project and M2M IoT project its completion, why is it that hardly any one uses it in information systems related M2M IoT projects?

1080. What is the unit of forecast value?

1081. How does this compare with other M2M IoT projects?

1082. Where are your problem areas?

1083. Verification is a process of ensuring that the developed system satisfies the stakeholders agreements and specifications; Are you building the product right? What do you verify?

4.4 Risk Audit: M2M IoT

1084. Do you have a consistent repeatable process that is actually used?

1085. How can the strategy fail/achieved?

1086. Are contracts reviewed before renewal?

1087. Are procedures in place to ensure the security of staff and information and compliance with privacy legislation if applicable?

1088. Has everyone (staff, volunteers and participants) agreed to a code of behaviour or conduct?

1089. Do staff understand the extent of their duty of care?

1090. Do you have written and signed agreements/ contracts in place for each paid staff member?

1091. Is the organization willing to commit significant time to the requirements gathering process?

1092. Management -what contingency plans do you have if the risk becomes a reality?

1093. Auditor independence: A burdensome constraint or a core value?

1094. Do you have a mechanism for managing change?

1095. Will an appropriate standard of care be applied to all involved?

1096. Is your organization an exempt employer for payroll tax purposes?

1097. What is happening in other jurisdictions? Could that happen here?

1098. How do you manage risk?

1099. Does Willful Intent Modify Risk-Based Auditing?

1100. Have you considered the health and safety of everyone in the organization and do you meet work health and safety regulations?

1101. What resources are needed to achieve program results?

1102. Improving Fraud Detection: Do Auditors React to Abnormal Inconsistencies between Financial and Non-financial Measures?

1103. How risk averse are you?

4.5 Contractor Status Report: M2M IoT

1104. What are the minimum and optimal bandwidth requirements for the proposed soluiton?

1105. What was the budget or estimated cost for your companys services?

1106. How long have you been using the services?

1107. Are there contractual transfer concerns?

1108. What was the final actual cost?

1109. What was the actual budget or estimated cost for your companys services?

1110. Describe how often regular updates are made to the proposed solution. Are these regular updates included in the standard maintenance plan?

1111. How is Risk Transferred?

1112. What is the average response time for answering a support call?

1113. If applicable; describe your standard schedule for new software version releases. Are new software version releases included in the standard maintenance plan?

1114. What was the overall budget or estimated cost?

1115. What process manages the contracts?

1116. Who can list a M2M IoT project as company experience, the company or a previous employee of the company?

4.6 Formal Acceptance: M2M IoT

1117. What lessons were learned about your M2M IoT project management methodology?

1118. What are the requirements against which to test, Who will execute?

1119. Do you buy pre-configured systems or build your own configuration?

1120. Does it do what client said it would?

1121. Who would use it?

1122. Did the M2M IoT project manager and team act in a professional and ethical manner?

1123. General estimate of the costs and times to complete the M2M IoT project?

1124. Did the M2M IoT project achieve its MOV?

1125. What is the Acceptance Management Process?

1126. Do you perform formal acceptance or burn-in tests?

1127. Was the M2M IoT project managed well?

1128. How well did the team follow the methodology?

1129. How does your team plan to obtain formal acceptance on your M2M IoT project?

1130. What can you do better next time?

1131. Was the M2M IoT project work done on time, within budget, and according to specification?

1132. What function(s) does it fill or meet?

1133. Was business value realized?

1134. Was the sponsor/customer satisfied?

1135. Does it do what M2M IoT project team said it would?

1136. Do you buy-in installation services?

5.0 Closing Process Group: M2M IoT

1137. Contingency planning. If a risk event occurs, what will you do?

1138. Were risks identified and mitigated?

1139. Did you do what you said you were going to do?

1140. Is there a clear cause and effect between the activity and the lesson learned?

1141. What were the desired outcomes?

1142. Based on your M2M IoT project communication management plan, what worked well?

1143. What areas were overlooked on this M2M IoT project?

1144. If action is called for, what form should it take?

1145. What Will You Do?

1146. How dependent is the M2M IoT project on other M2M IoT projects or work efforts?

1147. Did the M2M IoT project team have the right skills?

1148. Will the M2M IoT project deliverable(s) replace a current asset or group of assets?

1149. Were escalated issues resolved promptly?

1150. How critical is the M2M IoT project success to the success of the organization?

1151. Were the outcomes different from those planned?

1152. Is this a follow-on to a previous M2M IoT project?

5.1 Procurement Audit: M2M IoT

1153. Is the strategy implemented across the entire organization?

1154. Are payment generated from computer programs reviewed by supervisory personnel prior to distribution?

1155. Are criteria and sub-criteria set suitable to identify the tender that offers best value for money?

1156. Could the bidders assess the economic risks the successful bidder would be responsible for, thus limiting the inclusion of extra charges for risk?

1157. Were there no material changes in the contract shortly after award?

1158. Did you consider and evaluate alternatives, like bundling needs with other departments or grouping supplies in separate lots with different characteristics?

1159. Are all purchase orders signed by the purchasing agent?

1160. Is the procurement process organized the most appropriate way taking into consideration the amount of procurement?

1161. Where an electronic auction was used to bid, were all required specifications given equally to tenderers?

1162. Are purchase orders pre-numbered?

1163. Does an appropriately qualified official check the quality of performance against the contract terms?

1164. Are buyers prohibited from accepting gifts from vendors?

1165. Was the award criterion only the most economical advantageous tender?

1166. Is the issuance of purchase orders scheduled so that orders are not issued daily?

1167. Are all mutilated and voided checks retained for proper accounting of pre-numbered checks?

1168. Budget controls: Does your organization maintain an up-to-date (approved) budget for all funded activities, and perform a comparison of that budget with actual expenditures for each budget category?

1169. Were additional deliveries a partial replacement for normal supplies or installations or an extension of existing supplies or installations?

1170. In open and restricted procedures, did the contracting authority make sure that there is no substantive change to the bid due to this clearing process?

1171. Was the award criteria that of the most economically advantageous tender?

1172. Has it been determined which areas of procurement the audit should cover?

5.2 Contract Close-Out: M2M IoT

1173. Have all acceptance criteria been met prior to final payment to contractors?

1174. How does it work?

1175. Have all contracts been completed?

1176. Why Outsource?

1177. Have all contract records been included in the M2M IoT project archives?

1178. Parties: Authorized?

1179. A change in knowledge?

1180. A change in circumstances?

1181. Was the contract sufficiently clear so as not to result in numerous disputes and misunderstandings?

1182. Has each contract been audited to verify acceptance and delivery?

1183. How is the contracting office notified of the automatic contract close-out?

1184. What happens to the recipient of services?

1185. Are the signers the authorized officials?

1186. Was the contract complete without requiring

numerous changes and revisions?

1187. Parties: Who is Involved?

1188. Have all contracts been closed?

1189. What is Capture Management?

1190. Was the contract type appropriate?

1191. A change in attitude or behavior?

1192. How/When Used ?

5.3 Project or Phase Close-Out: M2M IoT

1193. What process was planned for managing issues/ risks?

1194. What can you do better next time, and what specific actions can you take to improve?

1195. What benefits or impacts does the stakeholder group expect to obtain as a result of the M2M IoT project?

1196. Who controlled the resources for the M2M IoT project?

1197. Complete Yes or No?

1198. What is a Risk Management Process?

1199. Did the delivered product meet the specified requirements and goals of the M2M IoT project?

1200. In addition to assessing whether the M2M IoT project was successful, it is equally critical to analyze why it was or was not fully successful. Are you including this?

1201. Was the user/client satisfied with the end product?

1202. Planned Remaining Costs?

1203. What were the actual outcomes?

1204. What information is each stakeholder group interested in?

1205. What could have been improved?

1206. What advantages do the an individual interview have over a group meeting, and vice-versa?

1207. What information did each stakeholder need to contribute to the M2M IoT projects success?

1208. What are the marketing communication needs for each stakeholder?

1209. In preparing the Lessons Learned report, should it reflect a consensus viewpoint, or should the report reflect the different individual viewpoints?

1210. If you were the M2M IoT project sponsor, how would you determine which M2M IoT project team(s) and/or individuals deserve recognition?

1211. What could be done to improve the process?

5.4 Lessons Learned: M2M IoT

1212. Does the lesson describe a function that would be done differently the next time?

1213. How actively and meaningfully were stakeholders involved in the M2M IoT project?

1214. Was the M2M IoT project manager sufficiently experienced, skilled, trained, supported?

1215. How well were expectations met regarding the frequency and content of information that was conveyed to by the M2M IoT project Manager?

1216. How was the quality of products/processes assured?

1217. How effective was the quality assurance process?

1218. What was helpful to know when planning the deployment?

1219. Overall, how effective were the efforts to prepare you and your organization for the impact of the product/service of the M2M IoT project?

1220. Was any formal risk assessment carried out at the start of the M2M IoT project, and was this followed up during the M2M IoT project?

1221. Was sufficient time allocated to review M2M IoT project deliverables?

1222. What were the main sources of frustration in the M2M IoT project?

1223. Was the purpose of the M2M IoT project, the end products and success criteria clearly defined and agreed at the start?

1224. Under what legal authority did the organization head and program manager direct the organization and M2M IoT project?

1225. Is there any way in which you think our development process hampered this M2M IoT project?

1226. How effective was the acceptance management process?

1227. How was the M2M IoT project controlled?

1228. How well were M2M IoT project issues communicated throughout your involvement in the M2M IoT project?

1229. How well prepared were you to receive M2M IoT project deliverables?

1230. How effective were the communications materials in providing and orienting team members about the details of the M2M IoT project?

1231. What are your lessons learned that you will keep in mind for the next M2M IoT project you participate in?

Index

242

Lightning Source UK Ltd.
Milton Keynes UK
UKHW010741050119
334993UK00011B/660/P